# MOTIVE POWER REVIEW

## EDITED BY REX KENNEDY

Network SouthEast-liveried Class 50
No 50026 *Indomitable* on the up fast
line at Pangbourne with the 13.00
Oxford-Paddington on 7 July 1988.
*Brian Perryman*

LONDON
IAN ALLAN LTD

First published 1989

ISBN 0 7110 1867 7



© Ian Allan Ltd 1989

Published by Ian Allan Ltd, Shepperton, Surrey; and printed by Ian Allan Printing Ltd at their works at Coombelands in Runnymede, England

Front cover:
**The Brush Class 89 prototype No 89001 at Rugby on a test working on 28 April 1987.** *Chris Morrison*

Back cover, top:
**Class 142 'Skipper' DMU No 142015 in chocolate and cream livery pauses at Preston with the 11.10 Blackpool North-Liverpool Lime Street service on 21 May 1988.** *John E. Oxley*

Back cover, bottom:
**Railfreight Class 47/3 No 47317 winds its way past Claverton with the 14.40 Salisbury-Gloucester service on 11 April 1988.** *Peter J. Robinson*

Below:
**On display at Doncaster station on 3 July 1988 was Class 89 No 89001, now named *Avocet*, beside Class 91 No 91003. This view clearly shows the blunt-ended No 2 cab of the Class 91 locomotive.** *Peter Harris*

# Contents

# Introduction

During 1987 and 1988 many interesting events occurred on British Rail. We have lost certain locomotive classes, and motive power depots and yards have been taken out of use, but a great deal of interest has been created by new locomotive and multiple-unit classes and new projects such as work on the Channel Tunnel. The Railfreight Sector has taken on a new look, and an increasing number of attractive liveries are now to be seen on locomotives and multiple-units throughout Britain.

Every day on BR something of importance is happening, and every railway enthusiast has his own particular favourite area of interest, whether it be a location, a class of locomotive or unit, or a certain type of traffic.

Obviously it would be impossible to cover all the events which have taken place on BR over the period under review in the limited space available, but I have endeavoured to cater for the tastes of all. Many of the facts have, of course been quoted in the various railway magazines, but this book sets out to provide the reader with a more permanent reminder of the events of the period as well as taking a look at future events. In addition, the book has been compiled such that there is a certain connection, sometimes small, between the chapters in an endeavour to create a flow of interest for the reader.

Every year we mourn the loss of something on BR, but we welcome that which replaces it most of the time. But to enthusiasts certain things are irreplaceable, like the 'Peaks', but the preservation movement takes over from BR and we must recognise the efforts of those hard-working lads involved in such ventures.

New stations open, but today very few close — what a different story to that of the 1960s — and the smart Sprinters are in abundance where electrification cannot be found.

In compiling this book I would like to thank a very special dependable friend, Brian Morrison, for his help in providing many of the pictures and certain information (yet again!) — thank you, Brian.

Both as a railway enthusiast and on account of the occasion, my happiest memory involving rail travel in Britain concerned the 'Orient Express Christmas Lunch Special' of 6 December 1988, which departed from Victoria station behind Class 73/1 No 73105 *Quadrant* for a 3½hr journey, including a round trip via Canterbury, Ramsgate and Ashford. On that occasion a lovely lady became my fiancée, and we were spoilt to say the least. I was very glad that I had not taken the car as driving home would have been out of the question! The Class 442 unit on which we travelled back home to Bournemouth seemed quite 'downmarket' after wining and dining in the unsurpassed luxury of those magnificent Pullman coaches.

*Rex Kennedy*
*December 1988*

Below:
**VSOE organised various excursions during 1988 to places such as Royal Ascot, Bournemouth and Leeds Castle in Kent, in addition to the Christmas Lunch specials which ran from Victoria in December. On 28 May 1988, Class 73/1 No 73126 is pictured at Deepcut, between Brookwood and Farnborough, on one of the Bournemouth specials, hauling the fine chocolate and cream-liveried coaches.** *John Scrace*

# 1
# BR Traction Review 1987/88

During 1987 and throughout 1988, BR has withdrawn more of our old favourites from revenue-earning service. However, most are not entirely extinct as some locomotives have entered Departmental service stock and others have been added to the preservation list. Greatly reduced are the Class 03 shunters, and gone are the '25s', '27s', and 'Peaks' to be replaced by the futuristic Class 89, 90 and 91 electrics as BR looks ahead into the 21st century. On the multiple-unit scene, Sprinters are taking over with a vengeance on non-electrified lines, while the Class 105 Cravens DMUs have all but disappeared. The Class 319, 321 and the Class 442 'Wessex Electric' EMUs have introduced us to modern design standards with great comfort and on-board facilities.

New liveries have been introduced on passenger stock, including the InterCity 'Swallow' scheme and the sub-Sector dedication of locomotives has resulted in six new livery varieties within the Railfreight fleet.

Class 37 has undergone major changes with sub-Classes 37/3, 37/5, 37/7, and 37/9 being created by the modification of certain Class 37/0s. A Railfreight Sector Class 50 briefly emerged, No 50149 *Defiance*, and 12 Class 73/1 electro-diesels were specifically dedicated for 'Gatwick Express' duties but not solely used on them. The two Class 210 diesel-electric multiple-units (DEMUs) have been disbanded, with four cars finding re-use in the Class 457 EMUs which have been formed as testbeds for the forthcoming Class 465 'Networker' EMU — the commuter train of the 1990s.

These are just some of the changes which have taken place during the 1987/88 period and this brief review hopefully will provide both nostalgia and an insight into the new traction which has graced BR metals during the period.

## Withdrawn Locomotives

### Class 03

By the end of 1988 the Class 03 shunter fleet had been reduced to just four after about 30 years in service. By late June 1987, the Norwich allocation had been reduced to one, No 03089 temporarily retained for work at Ipswich Docks. Norwich's other '03s' were sent to March for scrap rather

Below:
**One of the three Class 03 shunters based at Birkenhead, No 03170, is seen shunting a 'Grainflow' hopper wagon at Birkenhead on the Mersey Docks & Harbour Board lines on 8 July 1987.**
*Tom Heavyside*

than being transferred, thus signifying the end of the line for the East Anglian stalwarts. Gateshead's '03s' continued in service until January 1988. The withdrawn Gateshead allocation was not a problem as Class 08s could replace them there, but at Birkenhead the '08s' were not really suitable for dock work due to a weight restriction over Duke Street Bridge, connecting Birkenhead with Wallasey, leaving their three Class 03s still in service at the end of December 1988. In contrast to the present situation, the end of November 1987 saw six members of the class remaining — Nos 03066/78 at Newcastle Central, No 03094 out of use at Gateshead, and Nos 03073/162/170 at Birkenhead Docks.

On 30 June 1988, ex-Ipswich Docks No 03179 was sent to the Isle of Wight and has been modified with a cut-down cab and Network SouthEast livery at Ryde depot. At present, No 03079 is still being used on the Island. However, we shall no doubt see these fascinating locomotives working at industrial locations for some time to come as many have been sold for private industry. Even Mayer Newman of Snailwell, Newmarket has been using No 03020 to help move scrap metal from cut-up BR stock, and by October 1988 the Class 03 shunter became Britain's most prolific preserved diesel class with 25 examples being found in private ownership.

## Class 25

During March 1987, the Class 25 diesels ceased to operate in BR service. Originally allocated to the London Midland Region (LMR) these 1,250hp Type 2 Bo-Bos also came to be maintained at non-LMR depots such as Finsbury Park, March, Colwick, Wath, Neville Hill, Haymarket, Hither Green, Bristol Bath Road, Cardiff, Laira and Newport. Withdrawals started in 1976 when 10 were taken out of service, and from 1980 to 1987 between 20 and 56 locomotives were withdrawn each year.

Late in 1985, 12 Class 25/3s were reclassified '25/9' and renumbered 25901-12 for Chemicals sub-Sector duties based at Carlisle, and were restricted to a maximum speed of 60mph.

Nos 25310/05/14 were converted at Aberdeen Ferryhill to Electric Train Heat Ex-Locomotives, were numbered ETHEL 1, 2 and 3 respectively (running Nos 97250/51/52) and were used for stock-heating purposes prior to the conversion of the eth-equipped Class 37/4s for service on the West Highland line. On their redundancy two were used to provide electric heating of stock on preserved steam locomotive-hauled trains. No 97250 saw a brief period of use at Derby Carriage Works but asbestos insulation precluded its retention. Locomotive No 25912 had a double claim to fame. It was withdrawn, overhauled by Tyseley TMD apprentices and on final withdrawal went to Leeds Holbeck as a training locomotive. Fortunately, preserved Class 25s exist in abundance and include Nos 25035/057/059/067/072/083/176/191/244/265/278/279/313/904 and 909.

The image that will always remain in the minds of admirers of the class was the scene at Vic Berry's scrapyard at Leicester in July 1988, where Class 25 bodyshells were stacked in a three-tier pyramid awaiting breaking up — a sad, but spectacular sight.

## Class 27

The Class 27 'MacRats' ended their BR revenue-earning days in August 1987, Nos 27014/022/030/049/051/056/066/206 passing to Vic Berry at Leicester during September. The last Class 27 in service was No 27008. These locomotives will be remembered for their association with the Highland lines, and for their push-pull work on the Glasgow (Queen Street) to Edinburgh (Waverley) service, an operation which required the conversion of 12 members of the class from '27/1' to '27/2' in 1974/75, as a stopgap measure prior to the Class 47/7 conversions being used over this route. Originally, the Class 27s fell

Above:
**By 14 July 1987, when this scene was captured, few Class 27 locomotives remained in service. This view shows No 27066 marshalling a permanent way train at Kilwinning, junction for the line to Largs.** *Bert Wynn*

into three categories — those for Scottish Region (ScR) operation and fitted with single tablet catchers for working over single-line routes, those without train heating boilers which went to Thornaby, and the standard type which operated from Cricklewood. By the end of 1965, the nine Thornaby-based machines had been transferred to Toton and Wellingborough, and by 1968 these worked from Toton only, together with the ex-Cricklewood-based members of the class. By the time withdrawals began, all Class 27 locomotives had been allocated to ScR depots for some time.

Their Highland lines duties were taken over from 1978 by Class 37s, themselves soon to be replaced by Sprinter units. The routes to Oban, Mallaig, The Kyle of Lochalsh, Wick and Thurso will not seem the same without locomotive-hauled trains — and the '27s' will be especially missed.

Preserved examples include Nos 27001/07/50/59, No 27050 (ex-No 27106) being preserved on the Strathspey Railway as No D5394 in original two-tone green livery.

## Class 40

One of the favourites with diesel enthusiasts, the Class 40 'Whistlers' ended their BR days with the final run of No D200 from London (Liverpool Street) to York via Norwich on 16 April 1988. This run followed various problems with the locomotive's tyres, which had resulted in the cancellation of various previously-arranged railtours. It carried out its final duty in BR green livery, having operated some railtours in grey primer from 5-12 March. Its last run was a great success, following the route from London-Norwich as on its inaugural run of 18 April 1958. It even carried a similar headboard — only this time it read 'Last 2,000hp Diesel London-Norwich', and not 'First' as it had 30 years earlier. No D200 eventually came to rest in the afternoon on the turntable at the National Railway Museum at York — a most fitting resting place.

The Class 40 diesels have worked many duties during their lives, from the 'Royal Scot' to engineering trains. Predominantly working in the north-west, they will be remembered especially for their appearances on the Settle & Carlisle route, No D200 working its last timetabled passenger services over this line in 1987. It also worked various freight duties on the LMR during late 1987.

No D200 outlasted its brethren in revenue-earning service by over three years, although 1985 had seen four previously-withdrawn locomotives reinstated into Departmental service for the Crewe remodelling scheme and subsequent duties.

## Class 45

After various decision changes regarding the final withdrawal of the Class 45 'Peaks' in 1988, due to fluctuating shortages of motive power, their operational days on BR ended in July 1988, with the exception of No 45106 which was repainted in BR green livery and used on St Pancras to Derby commuter services and enthusiast charters until its untimely demise early in 1989.

The Class 45 'Peaks' were built at both Derby and Crewe and were introduced from 1960. They always looked smart in their green livery with a powder blue band. Although predominantly on the LMR and ER, they found themselves working to the West Country in their latter days. The majority of the class was withdrawn from Tinsley depot (the others from Toton) and from July 1986 many

Below:
During 1985, four Class 40 locomotives were given an extended lease of life and transferred to Departmental stock for use in connection with the track and signalling modifications at Crewe. These locomotives were numbered 97405 to 97408. The first to be withdrawn was No 97408 which is pictured on 12 February 1988 outside Crewe diesel depot, together with No 213 which had carried the number 40013 and the name *Andania*.
*Brian Morrison*

Bottom:
After its final run from Liverpool Street to York, and still sporting the special headboard, No D200 is seen outside the old York MPD, which is now the National Railway Museum's store and workshop, on 15 September 1988, five months after arriving.   *Brian Morrison*

D200
Pendennis
LAST
2000hp DIES
LONDON-NORW
progress by INTERC

HILLS &
CITIES
TOUR

could be seen in Vic Berry's scrapyard at Leicester awaiting the cutter's torch.

During their last two years of service, unofficial names started to appear on some of the remaining Class 45 'Peaks', such as *Pegasus*, *Apollo*, and *Zephyr* — an operation carried out at Tinsley, their final home. No D100 *Sherwood Forester* was privately purchased and restored to its former glory in green livery, and has appeared at BR open days throughout Britain.

Looking back at the withdrawal of the class, by July 1987 there were 14 Class 45/0s and 18 Class 45/1s still in service, six of these being condemned by 4 August 1987. At this time Class 45/0s were still occasionally to be found working passenger duties albeit without train-heating facilities.

By October 1987, reinstatement of certain withdrawn Class 45s was authorised for Departmental use in connection with electrification work on the East Coast main line (ECML); these were renumbered 97409-13 and based at Thornaby, although they were maintained at Tinsley.

Into 1988 the 'Peaks' could still be found at St Pancras on both passenger and parcels duties. No 45140 *Mercury* was even called upon to haul the first 'Wessex Electric' Class 442 unit from Derby to Brent Sidings, Cricklewood, on 29 January 1988! One of the regular 'Peak' duties, the newspaper trains, ceased on 10 July 1988, not helping the Class 45 survival situation, although in the same month they had a 'stay of execution' as BR decided to continue to use these expensive-to-maintain locomotives, with at least two Class 45/1s being reinstated. However, this decision was reversed by the end of the month. One of the last regular 'Peak' passenger workings was the Fridays-only 18.20 service from St Pancras to Derby, a working that remained locomotive-hauled (by Classes 37 and 47) even after the general withdrawal of the 'Peaks'.

Right:

**Two Class 105 Cravens DMUs, including Stratford's green-liveried set comprising vehicles Nos 53359 and 54122, were used to work the 'Vectis Velocipede' railtour from Stevenage to Portsmouth Harbour for the Ryde, Isle of Wight, Open Day, on 21 June 1986. The formation is pictured approaching Guildford on the outward trip.**
*Chris Wilson*

Thus 1988 saw the end of an era much loved by railway enthusiasts, especially those who remember these locomotives pounding up the Lickey Incline and over the West Country banks.

## Class 105 'Cravens' DMU

By December 1988, apart from the celebrated green-liveried two-car Class 105 set allocated to Norwich (Nos 53359/54122), very few remained. These included one car at Newton Heath, No 53812 (in poor condition), and six allocated to Cambridge for Parcels Sector duties. The green unit regularly worked Lowestoft trains in 1988, but on 20 June it was promoted to main line duty when it operated a Birmingham to Norwich service which was, at the time, a Class 156 Sprinter duty. The Craven DMUs were introduced in 1957, enjoying a career spanning more than 30 years.

## Class 202 and 203 'Hastings' DEMUs

The unusual 'Hastings' units with their 'slim-line' bodies have always created a great deal of interest with enthusiasts. No 203001 was turned out in green livery at Eastleigh Works in early July 1987 and together with the only other 'Hastings' survivor, No 202001, operated railtours to places such as Dover and Weymouth during the summer of 1987. On 12 September 1987, DMBS No 60014 of unit No 203001 was officially named *St Leonards* at that depot prior to working a staff outing to Weymouth. Sadly, the October 1987 storms damaged unit No 203001 but fortunately repairs were authorised and were carried out at Selhurst. In January 1988, the six-car unit, No 202001, was re-formed as a four-car set and reclassified '203/1', the two redundant coaches being used for spares, but its life was short and it was withdrawn from service by March 1988, leaving No 203001 as the sole 'Hastings' unit in revenue-earning service.

A preservation group has expressed interest in purchasing some vehicles for further use.

Left:

**Green-liveried Class 203 'Hastings' DEMU No 203001, named *St Leonards* at the depot of the same name on 12 September 1987, lies stabled at Eastbourne on 5 March 1988.**
*Melville Holley*

Above:
**Class 457 'Networker'
testbed EMU No 7001 was put to
work on scheduled services in November 1988
and is seen here at Waterloo on 5 December 1988
with the 14.43 to Windsor & Eton Riverside.** *Brian Morrison*

Below right:
**The second 'Networker' testbed unit, formed from Class 455/9 No 5920, is
pictured inside Strawberry Hill depot on 30 October 1988.** *Brian Morrison*

## Conversions and Modifications

### *Class 210 to Class 457 — DEMU to EMU*

The two Class 210 prototype DEMUs, introduced in 1982, were withdrawn from passenger service late in 1987. No 210001 was a four-car set and No 210002 comprised three cars. Originally, No 210001 operated from Reading and, after use in the West Midlands, No 210002 worked from Southall from late 1983. Following the closure of Southall depot, both units worked local services between Reading and Bedwyn.

In July 1987, No 210001 travelled to Derby RTC for conversion into the Class 457 EMU, a testbed for the forthcoming Class 465 'Networker' EMUs. At the time, No 210002 continued in traffic, eventually arriving at Derby to join its sister unit in January 1988. On 20 June 1988, the first Class 457 arrived at Strawberry Hill depot, and featured new seating and a trailer car from Class 455/8 unit No 5920. The new Class 457 four-car unit, No 7001, was hauled to Strawberry Hill by Class 50 No 50008 *Thunderer*.

We look forward to seeing the 'Networkers' in service, providing new standards on Network SouthEast services in the 1990s.

## Defiance — *50049 to 50149*

In July 1987, no decision had been made as to whether it would be No 50043 *Eagle* or No 50049 *Defiance* which would be fitted with Class 37/7-style bogies and allocated to the Railfreight Sector, but it was to be the latter which was sent to Laira T&RSMD in August for conversion to Class 50/1 specification. The conversion was intended to produce a locomotive with the load-starting characteristics of a Class 56, and which would be capable of handling the stone and ballast workings currently operated by pairs of Class 33s. By 16 September 1987 work had been completed on the two-month project, and the locomotive's first task, on 20 September, was a light engine movement from Laira to Newton Abbot to collect No 50012 *Benbow* which had been in collision with Skipper DMU No 14026. The conversion entailed various modifications to the basic Class 50 specification, not least of which was the fitting of CP7 bogies which are lower geared than the standard Class 50 type. Other modifications included derating the power unit to 2,450hp, and the application of new Railfreight livery complete with a yellow background to the nameplates.

Performance of the locomotive was uneven. Following a bad start on 23 September when No 50149 suffered a minor main generator flashover while climbing Hemerdon bank, it underwent extensive testing in October which included numerous adhesion trials on Warminster bank. However, performance of No 50149 was found to be little better than that of a standard Class 50 and, following a power-unit change, the locomotive worked in the Exeter area and eventually moved to Cornwall where it was put to work on china clay trains as a substitute for a damaged Class 37/5 locomotive. No 50149 was then allocated to Departmental duties at Gloucester and was banned from all exhibitions and railtours owing to its lack of availability, since when it was not on Departmental duties, it was required for maintenance. In March 1989 the locomotive was converted back to standard specification as No 50049.

### New Motive Power

### *Class 155 and 156 Super Sprinters*

On 4 August the first Leyland Bus-built Class 155 Sprinter arrived at Cardiff Canton, after trials, from the Derby Railway Technical Centre (RTC) to carry out two days of trials in the area, and the units commenced operation of Cardiff to Birmingham services from 5 October. Also during October 1987, the first Class 155 Sprinter on a Birmingham to Cambridge train appeared, substituting for a Class 150/1 and by early 1988 the Class 155s had increased their sphere of operation. By February they were becoming a common sight in North Wales.

By November 1987, the Provincial Sector's first Metro-Cammell Class 156 had made its debut, working trials between Tyseley and Banbury. By the new year, Class 156 No 156402 had arrived at Norwich for crew training, and these units are now used on services from there to Birmingham,

Below:
**During the period that it was working stone trains from Meldon quarry, Class 50/1 No 50149 *Defiance* is seen stabled at Exeter St Davids on the night of 5 November 1987.** *Colin J. Marsden*

Left:
**On 29 December 1987, Class 155 Leyland-built Sprinter No 155306 is seen leaving Kidderminster forming the 13.32 service from Birmingham New Street to Great Malvern.**
*Brian Morrison*

Right:
**While working a special round trip to March to introduce the new Sprinters to the line, Metro-Cammell Class 156 No 156404 leaves Ely station on 25 March 1988 with technical press and media representatives on board.**
*Brian Morrison*

Manchester and Blackpool. Scotland was next with No 156402 again working trial runs over a large area. ScotRail fitted mini-snowploughs to West Highland line Sprinters when the Class 37/4s ended their term of duty in January 1989.

The first revenue-earning Class 156 Sprinter working took place on 31 March 1988 and was an additional train from Derby to Lincoln Central forming a relief to the late-running 16.06 from Birmingham. On 30 April, Class 155 No 155310 joined forces with Class 156 units Nos 156401/03 on an excursion from The Wirral. Class 156 units commenced timetabled services on 16 May 1988 from Birmingham, Norwich, Liverpool Lime Street, Manchester, Blackpool, Derby and Cambridge — 16 units carrying out these duties — and 31 Class 155 Sprinters were based at Cardiff for the new summer timetable services. It was not long before one of the new units was involved in an incident, and on 8 June the first Class 156 Sprinter to be repaired, No 156410, arrived at Doncaster following a collision. As and when available, Class 156 Sprinters found their way to Norwich and Heaton depots, and July brought the first of the seven West Yorkshire PTE Class 155/1 units to Neville Hill to work on York-Manchester-Preston-Blackpool services.

The Sprinters had arrived with a vengeance!

## Class 456 EMUs

For use on the Guildford-Woking-Weybridge line, the Windsor-Staines-Richmond-Putney route and the Effingham Junction-Leatherhead-Epsom services are 24 new two car Class 456 EMUs ordered from BREL during the summer of 1988. These new units, similar in design to the Class 455s, should ease overcrowding at peak periods on these services which start from Waterloo. This move makes it possible to transfer 22 four-car Class 455 units from South-west inner suburban routes to Inner South Central services. These new units will allow demand and supply to be more closely matched through the operation of two-car trains during the off-peak period when there is insufficient demand to justify the use of a four-car unit. The new Class 456 units are due to be delivered in late 1990.

## Driving Van Trailers

The Driving Van Trailers (DVTs), converted from HST power cars, emerged from the Derby RTC in November 1987. The first two cars converted were Nos 43014 and 43123, and they were initially tested in conjunction with Class 86/2s No 86228 *Vulcan Heritage* and No 86240 *Bishop Eric Treacy* which had been fitted with Time Division Multiplex (TDM) equipment for push-pull operation.

Modifications to the power cars included the installation of conventional buffers and couplings. The power units were disconnected on the first conversions but were later reconnected, allowing the DVTs to work as conventional power cars if required.

Newly-converted DVT No 43013 was also used on the Class 89-hauled King's Cross-Peterborough trains in July 1988. The Class 43 engines are required to provide train equipment power since electric locomotives are not electrically compatible with IC125 stock.

The first of the Mk 3 DVTs for WCML duties, No 82101, was completed at BREL Derby Litchurch Lane in October 1988. Following type approval at Derby RTC the vehicle began testing on the Southern end of WCML.

Below:
**On 8 November 1988, Derby-built Driving Van Trailer (DVT) No 82101 was seen travelling at speed through Bushey at the rear of a test working from Wembley to Glasgow, hauled by Class 90 No 90006. The train comprises Test Car *Prometheus* and three cars of the 'International' set.** *Brian Morrison*

## Class 89

As long ago as 6 August 1987, the experimental No 89001 hauled its first reported passenger service, a Holyhead-Euston train, from Crewe to Willesden. The locomotive had not been cleared to enter Euston station as, being 1½in higher than a Class 87 it exceeded the permitted loading gauge. The following day it returned to Crewe with a Freightliner train. From then on tests continued on the West Coast main line (WCML).

Whilst carrying out trials on the WCML, the locomotive conveyed not only Research Division officials from the RTC at Derby, but also, on one occasion, SNCF representatives from France who were interested in the locomotive in connection with the Channel Tunnel project. Its impressive performance pleased the SNCF delegates, especially its acceleration and lack of wheelslip on ascending Shap from a standing start halfway up the bank at Scout Green. Following these tests the locomotive was moved to Hornsey for crew training prior to trial runs on the ECML.

On 20 May 1988, No 89001 formed part of a convoy of BR motive power which travelled from Derby to Dover to be conveyed by the SNCF ferry *Nord Pas de Calais* across the Channel to Hamburg, where it was hoped that Brush would be able to secure orders from European buyers. On its return from Hamburg No 89001 ran trials on the ECML and its first use on GN passenger work occurred on 3 July 1988 when it hauled the 09.00 King's Cross-Scarborough special as far as Doncaster. From 15 July, No 89001 was used on the 07.18 Peterborough-King's Cross and 17.36 return working in conjunction with Class 43 No 43013, making excellent time on the schedule. On 12 August, No 89001 worked to Leeds, substituting for a Class 43, and was the first electric locomotive to haul a passenger service to this destination.



Below:
**Class 89 No 89001 is seen together with Class 90 No 90008 and Class 91 No 91003 at Derby RTC on 19 May 1988, prior to joining a convoy to Dover from where the exhibits for the Hamburg exhibition were taken across the Channel by the ferry *Nord Pas de Calais*.** *Brian Morrison*

Above:
**Pictured at Carlisle with ecs, Class 90 No 90002 is seen on 25 June 1988 after an evaluation trial run from Crewe. This view clearly displays the 3in-high numbers which were fashionable (happily only for a short period) during 1988, and the swallow emblem introduced in 1987 for InterCity locomotives.** *D. Stuart Lindsey*

## Class 90

The infamous Class 90 electric locomotive eventually emerged from the depths of Crewe Works on the afternoon of 31 October 1987, and then travelled to the Derby RTC. Tests were carried out on the Old Dalby test track on Friday 13 November!

Of the initial order for 29 locomotives, 25 were officially allocated to WCML InterCity services and four to the Railfreight Sector. A further 21 are scheduled for ECML services. By February 1988, five Class 90s were virtually complete, and tests on the WCML were by then well underway. Indeed, on 30 March 1988, the first Class 90 was named, No 90005 *Financial Times*, in a ceremony at Euston.

By June 1988 problems started to occur and delivery of more members of the class was suspended whilst teething troubles were sorted out. The problems were soon rectified, however, and test runs continued on the WCML. On 24 June two of the class, Nos 90004 and 90005, reached the ER at Bounds Green for a special test run on the ECML. It was to be 11 July before No 90003 worked the class' first timetabled passenger train when it joined Class 86/4 No 86413 *County of*

15

*Lancashire* on the 13.40 Blackpool-Euston train from Preston and, on 16 July, No 90004 worked a Freightliner service. By mid-August, regular Class 90-hauled services were working from Euston to the north and, by September, BR had officially accepted Nos 90001-09 after extensive testing.

At the time of writing, crew training was due on the GE lines in preparation for through Railfreight operation from the WCML.

## Class 91

On 12 February 1988 GEC's Class 91 'Electra' locomotive was paraded before invited guests at Crewe Works, two years after BR's order had been placed for a fleet of 31 locomotives for ECML work. Their traction motors are developed from those used in the Class 87 fleet as these have proved to be extremely reliable. A feature of these locomotives is the 'blunt' end of the No 2 cab.

On 17 March, No 91001 carried out tests on the Old Dalby test track, assisted by Class 47/4 No 47443 and, on 4 April, No 91002 commenced tests on the ECML to Peterborough. No 91003 was the member of the class chosen to go to Hamburg in May. In June more test runs were carried out on the ECML in conjunction with Class 43s, with No 91001 reaching a speed of 143mph on 23 June. In July, No 91001 underwent tests on Shap bank and, on 11 August, No 91004 reached Leeds with a 300-tonne load. A speed of 145mph was attained by No 91002 on the GN main line in an attempt to reach 150mph. What speeds can we expect from these powerhouses in the future?

Above:
**Carrying out trials on the Derby RTC's Old Dalby test track, between Melton Junction and Edwalton, on 25 March 1988, Class 91 No 91001 is seen with Class 47/4 No 47438 together with Test Coach *Prometheus* and Test Car No 2, both coaches being based at the RTC.**
*Dennis R. Wilkins*

Below:
**Having made an early morning run from King's Cross, Class 91 No 91002 prepares to return to the capital after running round its train of Mk 3 sleepers at Peterborough on 4 April 1988. The outward journey was made sharp end first, with the return needing to be blunt end first due to there being no turning facilities on the line.**
*Brian Morrison*

## Class 319 'Thameslink' EMUs

The Class 319 EMUs got off to a poor start on 19 August 1987 when the first unit booked to run from Derby to Strawberry Hill for commissioning, failed to make the journey because numerous technical faults found at York could not be rectified in time. The first Class 319 unit, No 319001, eventually arrived at Strawberry Hill on 4 September 1987. Testing was carried out on the Shepperton branch and No 319002 followed soon after.

By early December 1987, the 10th Class 319 had been delivered and, on 1 December, No 319005 worked the 06.49 Bedford-Moorgate service. Mid-January 1988 saw the Class 319s working only one daily Bedford service, although subsequent months saw the class gradually taking over the Bedford line timetable, until by mid-August 1988 enough Class 319s had been delivered to eliminate the use of Class 317s on the 'Bed-Pan' line.

Right:
**The workforce responsible for construction of the first Class 321 EMU at BREL York is in attendance as the official roll-out of No 321301 takes place for the press on 15 September 1988.**
*Brian Morrison*

Left:
**On 16 April 1988, Class 319 'Thameslink' EMUs Nos 319031 and 319033 formed an 11.14 additional service from Brighton to London Bridge, and are seen awaiting departure from the seaside terminus.**
*Chris Wilson*

## Class 321 'Anglia' EMUs

At the time of writing the newest form of motive power to be seen was the Class 321 EMU, effectively a single-voltage version of the Class 319, available as both 25kV overhead and 750V dc third-rail designs, the former for Anglia Region services and the latter for use on the SR's Kent services. No 321301 has undertaken extensive trials on the GN main line between Doncaster and Peterborough. Entry into passenger service began on the Anglia Region in January 1989 and Ilford EMD will be responsible for maintaining the initial order for 46 of these stylish new four-car units.

### Class 442 'Wessex Electric' EMUs

On 18 December 1987, BREL Derby officially handed over the first Class 442 'Wessex Electric' unit for the Weymouth electrification to Chris Green, Network SouthEast Sector Director.

The new five-car units incorporated public payphones, a public address system, seating for the disabled, catering facilities and aircraft-style seating to maximise passenger accommodation. First-class accommodation is in both compartment and open configuration. An important safety feature is the provision of electrically-operated plug doors, although some problems have been experienced with these in service. The first Class 442 unit, No 2401, arrived at Bournemouth depot on 30 January 1988 and began trial running to Waterloo although, owing to the stock's 'C3' loading gauge restriction, the units are not permitted to work into Platforms 1-6 and 16-21 at Waterloo.

Above:

**From the commencement of the Summer 1988 timetable, the Class 442 'Wessex Electrics' were introduced on Waterloo-Weymouth services. On certain trains, the two five-car sets were split at Southampton with the leading set working a fast train to Bournemouth and Weymouth, leaving the second set to operate an all-stations service to Bournemouth. In this view, a complete 10-car train is seen arriving at Bournemouth from Waterloo headed by unit No 2404.** *Rex Kennedy*

During these trial runs, 104mph was achieved between Woking and Basingstoke, a feat soon to be eclipsed as the delivery of further units saw test running at speeds of up to 110mph.

Deliveries were slow, and in April 1988 BR finally admitted that only four new 'Wessex Electrics' would be operational by the summer timetable, for which 24 units had originally been planned. During the first months of service, from the very first scheduled run, problems were experienced with the plug doors and with the uncoupling of units at Southampton on the westbound journey, with the result that trains often ran 30min late and the Southampton stop was sometimes extended to as much as 20min. From 13 June 1988 the guard was made responsible for door operation while faults were rectified on passenger control systems.

Unit No 2413 entered passenger service on 18 July 1988 to a slightly modified design pattern incorporating a lounge area and with reduced brakevan accommodation. By mid-September 1988, 15 Class 442 units were available to cover 12 diagrams on the Waterloo-Weymouth line, and at the commencement of the new timetable in October 1988, Nos 2402-20 had entered revenue-earning service. No 2401 was still undergoing final test running at the time. Now that they are in service, the '442s' offer excellent commuter comfort, and timings over the route are generally good — an important factor to businessmen in particular.

# 2

# London – All Change!

Various changes have taken place in the capital during 1987 and 1988, including major improvements to some stations, new forms of traction, voltage uprating, 'Thameslink', new London Underground stock and the highly successful Docklands Light Railway (DLR). In this brief summary, details of some of the many changes are given, with illustrations to provide a picture of the changing scene in London.

Below:
**On 10 July 1988, the 09.46 Poole-Waterloo train approaches the end of its journey, propelled by Class 73/1 electro-diesels Nos 73106 and 73105** *Quadrant.* **During the period of time when traction motors for the forthcoming Class 442 EMUs were being removed from the 4-REPs, two Class 73/1 locomotives provided the motive power to enable schedules to be met on Bournemouth services.**
*Brian Morrison*

## Waterloo

The Class 442 'Wessex Electrics' have arrived. After extensive trials, these futuristic new five-car units, running in pairs to Bournemouth and Weymouth, have made most of the other EMUs operating from Waterloo look outdated. The first scheduled passenger service operated by a Class 442 was the 06.04 Weymouth-Waterloo on the first day of the 1988 summer timetable. In addition to the Class 442s, the new Class 457, the testbed for the forthcoming Class 465 'Networker' EMU, emerged. By early 1991 the Class 465 units should start operating from Victoria and Charing Cross to Kent, and a 25kV version into Essex by late 1992 but, for testing purposes, the Class 457 'testbed' unit has been working on Windsor line suburban services out of Waterloo.

On the locomotive-hauled scene, prior to the 1988 summer timetable, Bournemouth trains were in the news again, with double-headed Class 73/1s substituting for 4-REP power as the latter's traction equipment was progressively removed for reuse in the Class 442 'Wessex Electrics', and three-car 'REP' formations appeared in multiple with 4-TC sets. Bournemouth line trains produced a variety of motive power combinations including nine-car and 13-car trains, generally being locomotive-hauled into Waterloo. Even the Class 423 4-VEPs are receiving a facelift and 'Gatwick Express'-allocated Class 73/2s were also to be found on Bournemouth trains during the spring of 1988. Class 415 and 416 'EPB' units were also seen at Waterloo during September 1988 due to shortages of stock on Network SouthEast's South Western lines.

## Victoria

On 1 December 1987, a mock-up of the Class 465 'Networker' EMU — the commuter train of the 1990s — was put on display at Victoria station.

On 21 December, two additional platforms were opened, Nos 16 and 17

**With its original number, 6580, restored to both the cab and bodyside, in addition to its TOPS number, No 33119 is seen having arrived at Waterloo after propelling the 13.15 service from Salisbury on 24 March 1988. Alongside is Class 423/4 4-VEP No 3421 (ex-No 3021), the first of the fleet to be refurbished. BRML Eastleigh has the contract for refurbishing the whole 4-VEP fleet, involving a complete interior strip-out with additional seating installed in lieu of guard's space. Numbers change from series 30XX to 34XX on completion of the work.** *Brian Morrison*

**On 20 September 1988, the 11.30 service to Weymouth leaves Waterloo worked by Class 442 'Wessex Electric' unit No 2411. By mid-September, deliveries of Class 442 EMUs to Bournemouth had reached No 2418, but as the first two were not passed for traffic and number 2418 itself was on commissioning tests, this left only 15 sets available to cover 12 diagrams.** *Brian Morrison*

and, on 4 January 1988, work commenced on a redevelopment project to provide a covered shopping area and modern offices above Platforms 9 to 19. Work started above Platforms 18 and 19, with trains consequently being moved to the new Platforms 16 and 17. Victoria will never look the same again. The 'Gatwick Express' service received a new look early in 1988 with refurbishment of the stock to match InterCity standards elsewhere, and the service even acquired its own Class 09 shunter in InterCity livery, No 09012 *Dick Hardy*. Twelve dedicated Class 73/1 electro-diesels were renumbered 73201-12 and roof-level mini numbers were positioned on the DMLV units. The DMLVs also lost their yellow cabsides.

## London Bridge

Class 319 'Thameslink' units first worked into the station when operating on test runs, in January 1988. These units now work regularly via London Bridge to Brighton and north to Bedford. The station even entertained a Class 442 'Wessex Electric' on 27 August 1988 when exhibits at the Steam & Model Railway Gala also included Classes 33, 56, 58, and 'Deltic' No D9000 *Royal Scots Grey*.

Above left:
**Forming the 16.17 Bedford to Moorgate train on 1 August 1988, Class 319 'Thameslink' units Nos 319042/034 ascend the incline into Farringdon station.** *Chris Wilson*

Left:
**A scene from the London Bridge station Gala Day on 27 August 1988 shows Class 58 No 58050 *Toton Traction Depot* in Railfreight Coal sub-Sector livery, displayed between a Class 442 'Wessex Electric' and de-icing EMU No 007.** *Brian Morrison*

## Thameslink

HRH The Princess Royal officially opened the new 'Thameslink' service at Blackfriars station on 25 April 1988. The new service, operated by Class 319 units, operates from Bedford in the north, via King's Cross Thameslink station (formerly King's Cross Midland City) to Blackfriars and thence to Brighton and other locations south of the Thames.

Major construction work on the Snow Hill tunnel was necessary in linking Farringdon with Blackfriars, utilising the original trackbed through the tunnel which was closed to passengers in 1916 and freight in 1968. The line emerges from the tunnel beside Holborn Viaduct station. Considering that the tunnel had been out of use for many years its condition was remarkably good.

It is intended to introduce new services via the reopened Snow Hill tunnel to other destinations in Kent, by creating a St Paul's Thameslink underground station, allowing the closure of Holborn Viaduct, and eventually linking with Channel Tunnel trains at the proposed Ashford International station in 1993.

## St Pancras

During 1988 the Class 45 locomotive-hauled workings from St Pancras declined in number although there was still at the time of writing one locomotive-hauled Derby train on a Friday evening, albeit sadly no longer 'Peak'-hauled. Late in 1988 motive power included Classes 37 and 47, and even Departmental Class 47 No 97545 put in some appearances, borrowed from RTC duties.

St Pancras entertained an unscheduled visitor on 27 December 1987 in the form of Class 154 Sprinter No 154001 working a relief service to Derby. In February 1988 this experimental unit was renumbered 154002 to avoid confusion with similar units. A new service started from St Pancras from 16 May 1988. This was the 'Yorkshire TPO' Travelling Post Office service which leaves for York and Newcastle to arrive in time for first deliveries in Yorkshire and County Durham.

St Pancras station is to be involved in a mammoth new redevelopment scheme, which includes King's Cross, scheduled to be completed by 1995 at a cost of £5 billion. The scheme would involve the creation of a new six-platform cross-London InterCity station with rail links to the Channel Tunnel and to Gatwick and Stansted airports. The Railway Development Society is amongst those who hope that this redevelopment will encourage BR to electrify the St Pancras to Sheffield route.

Below:
**The inaugural run of the 'Thameslink' service was staged on 25 April 1988 from Blackfriars station, following the official opening of the new link by HRH the Princess Royal who travelled to Crystal Palace in the first train with some 500 children in connection with Save the Children Week. The second train, containing the media, also travelled to Crystal Palace where it is seen here formed of units Nos 319031/ 033.** *Brian Morrison*

Right:
**St Pancras also sees 'Thameslink' Class 319 units in connection with the 'Bed-Pan' services to Bedford, particularly at weekends when the normal weekday service to Moorgate does not operate. On 26 June 1988, ecs to form the 00.50 train to Bedford stands overnight in St Pancras station, formed of unit No 319033.** *Brian Morrison*

Below right:
**On 23 February 1987, the Newcastle TPO service prepares to leave St Pancras hauled by Class 47/4 No 47537 *Sir Gwynedd/County of Gwynedd*.** *Michael J. Collins, BA*

Below:
**Class 319 'Thameslink' EMU No 319037 arrives at Elstree & Borehamwood with the 13.30 Sevenoaks-Luton on 30 May 1988.** *John E. Oxley*

Right:
**The last Class 45 'Peak' in service, No 45106, sporting green livery, prepares to leave St Pancras with the 17.50 InterCity service to Derby on 21 October 1988, the only locomotive-hauled service out of St Pancras apart from one Friday-only train hauled by a Class 37 or 47.** *Brian Morrison*

## King's Cross

Probably the most interesting event at King's Cross during 1988 involved the Class 89 and 91 locomotives, with the general public getting the full advantage of the efficient Class 89, No 89001, together with a Class 43 at the rear, on the evening run to Peterborough. However, a sad loss to King's Cross was the withdrawal of sleeper services over the ECML from May 1988, depriving important cities such as York and Newcastle of this service.

An interesting working occurred on 11 December 1987, when Class 86/4 No 86403 became the first of its class to work a passenger train out of King's Cross, when it was rostered to the 16.35 to Peterborough. In addition the stock was the West Highland line Mk 1 set in green and cream livery! By February 1988 the first of an additional build of Class 317/1 units for GN services had entered service between King's Cross and Peterborough, and on 2 May 1988, two weeks before the new summer timetable was due to commence, through workings, using Class 317 units, were introduced between Cambridge and King's Cross.

An unusual 'reopening' occurred at King's Cross during 1988 when the hitherto disused Platform 11 was reinstated and, to help smooth the flow of travellers using this busy station, routine ticket inspections at the barriers ceased, making it an 'open' station.

Right:
Due to a shortage of suitable EMUs on
the evening of 11 December 1987, the
16.35 King's Cross-Peterborough
service surprisingly consisted of Class
86/4 No 86403, two Motorail-allocated
Open First coaches and the eight-coach
'West Highland' Mk 1 set in its green
and cream livery. Apart from the
unusual coaching stock, this was the
first occasion that an electric
locomotive had worked a scheduled
passenger service from King's Cross.
Brian Morrison

Below:
The last occasion on which sleeper
stock was rostered to appear at King's
Cross was at the culmination of the
1987/88 winter timetable. The final duty
was specially allocated to Class 47/4
No 47401 (ex-D1500), the forerunner of
the type, although devoid of its North
Eastern nameplates which are now
carried by No 47443. In this view
No 47434 waits to take out the ecs.
Ken Brunt

Above:
**Class 317 EMUs took over the King's Cross-Royston services from Class 310 and 312 units during 1987. Electrification of the Royston-Cambridge line was followed in 1988 by Class 317 units working through to Cambridge. On 26 June 1988, the 13.45 to Cambridge awaits its departure time at King's Cross, illuminated by the attractive new station lamps.**
*Brian Morrison*

Left:
**A rare Class 90 working into King's Cross. On 27 June 1988, No 90005 *Financial Times* rests at the buffer-stops at 05.40 having brought in a test train which included sleeping cars from Grantham that had worked overnight between there and Peterborough.**
*Ken Brunt*

Below left:
**DVT No 43013 arrives at King's Cross on 15 July 1988 heading ecs to form the 17.35 to Peterborough. The train was hauled by No 89001, which is already attached to the stock at the tunnel end.** *Brian Morrison*

*Above:*
**Class 89 No 89001 prepares to depart from King's Cross with the 17.35 service to Peterborough referred to in the previous caption. This was the first occasion that the Class 89 was used by BR to haul a revenue-earning service. This diagram was worked by the locomotive until November 1988 when it was taken over by a Class 47, the '89' graduating to a Leeds diagram.**
*Brian Morrison*

## London Underground

The most horrific disaster ever on the London Underground occurred at King's Cross Underground station on 18 November 1987, when a major fire destroyed the station resulting in heavy loss of life. The judicial inquiry made numerous recommendations and major reconstruction work has taken place. The replacement of the wooden escalators has top priority.

New prototype 1990 Central Line and Victoria Line stock was put on view at Woodford on 8 June for one week. Liveries were light green and silver, blue and silver, red and silver for the Central Line units. These prototypes entered limited public service on 4 May 1988 at Stanmore, on the Jubilee Line. Each train consisted of two cars from each of the three types built resulting in a livery combination of blue, green and red — a colourful sight!

Before 1987 had ended, the first of 16 new London Underground trains had been delivered from Metro-Cammell, similar to those introduced on the Jubilee Line in 1983. The older 1983 stock will be cascaded to the Bakerloo, Northern, Central and Victoria lines.

Work started in 1988 on a major scheme to replace the lifts at Angel Underground station with escalators. The £20 million project, incorporating a new ticket hall, is due for completion by 1992. The scheme will also dispense with the island platform, producing a conventional two-platform layout.

*Below:*
**On 8 June 1987 the new prototype 1990 London Underground stock was on view at Woodford station. The three new liveries of light green, blue, and red were displayed to gauge public reaction. These trains entered service on 4 May 1988 on the Jubilee Line and comprised six cars in various colour schemes.** *Ken Cordner*

## Docklands Light Railway

On 30 July 1987, HM The Queen opened the Docklands Light Railway (DLR). The system comprises two lines from Island Gardens to West India Quay, from which one route passes through Limehouse to Tower Gateway, and the other runs to Bow and Stratford where it connects with BR and London Underground services. Initially, a pair of two-car trains operated these services. Public service began from Poplar, following initial problems with the computerised operation of the driverless trains, although these faults were soon rectified. A 'Train Captain' is on board for revenue protection, and he or she is capable of taking over as driver in an emergency. On the first day of service, 50,000 passengers were conveyed over this new railway.

Below:
**Docklands Light Railway (DLR) unit No 04 departs from West Ferry station working a service for Island Gardens on 31 August 1987, the first day of public service on the railway.** *Michael McGowan*

In March 1988, tunnelling commenced on the new extension to Bank — the first underground railway to be built in London for 80 years. It is hoped that the link will be complete by 1991. At first, DLR traffic levels stood at around 20,000 passengers per day, but by the mid-1990s, when the Isle of Dogs Canary Wharf scheme is complete, it is anticipated that around 66,000 passengers will use the DLR every day.

**Inside the Docklands Light Railway depot at Poplar on 30 July 1987, two of the GEC-built units, Nos 06 and 07, are seen on display for the official opening by Her Majesty the Queen.** *Brian Morrison*

## Liverpool Street

Extensive modernisation took place at Liverpool Street during 1988 in an effort to update the station for the 1990s. Liverpool Street-Cambridge services were operated by Class 310s from late 1987 and East Ham depot became responsible for maintenance. By late January 1988, eight Class 310 EMUs were available for Liverpool Street services and by 16 May, following the introduction of the new 1988 summer timetable, the Class 310 units had taken over the GE Liverpool Street-Southend Victoria services.

Right:
**Class 302 EMU No 302277 leaves Fenchurch Street station on 21 September 1987 forming the 10.30 stopping service to Shoeburyness, and passes sister unit No 302229 entering the station on the 09.26 working from Shoeburyness. The particular stretch of track seen in this view is scheduled for uprating from 6.25kV to 25kV and was due for completion in March 1989. The Class 302 units were constructed for dual-voltage operation.**  *Brian Morrison*

## Fenchurch Street

On 21 September 1987 the modernised Fenchurch Street station was officially opened by the Lord Mayor of London after three years of work. The rebuilding is part of a £28.5 million property development scheme in the area. The new facilities include new escalators, improved catering and electronic information display units. In April 1988, work started on the updating of the 6.25kV overhead electric supply from Fenchurch Street to East Ham on the Southend Central line, the work being scheduled for completion in March 1989 (see Chapter 3).

## Paddington

Through services now operate from Paddington to Greenford, generally using a Class 121 single-car DMU. Prior to the 1988 summer timetable, these trains operated between Ealing Broadway and Greenford only.

On 3 December 1987, Paddington saw its first Class 155 Sprinter when No 155309 worked a special from

Above:
**Services from Greenford to Ealing Broadway were extended to Paddington from the 1988 summer timetable, bringing Pressed Steel Co Class 121 single-car units ('bubble cars' as they are affectionately known) into the terminus on a regular basis. Nos 55023 and 55024 are seen forming the 11.36 Greenford-Paddington and the 11.40 Paddington-Greenford passing at Ealing Broadway on 7 September 1988.** *Brian Morrison*

Cholsey in connection with the 'Provincial Express' launch.

Paddington's Pullman services were increased from two to four daily from May 1988, incorporating the 'Red Dragon Pullman' to South Wales and the 'West Country Pullman' to Torbay. InterCity departures were increased to 69 per day.

## Euston

Many 'new faces' have appeared at Euston during the period under review, including Class 90 electrics,

Class 317 EMUs on Birmingham and Northampton local services, and overhauled Class 313 EMUs on the revamped 'Harlequin' local service to Watford Junction. Following a period of driver training over the route late in 1987, the Class 317s entered service from Euston during 1988, supplementing the Class 319 and 312 units already in service on the route. The Class 317s were maintained at Bletchley, having been transferred from the 'Bed-Pan' line at Cricklewood.

The first of the new 4,850hp Class 90 locomotives to haul a train conveying passengers worked out of Euston on 30 March 1988 with No 90005 in command following its official naming as *Financial Times* and, on 11 July, No 90003 arrived at Euston paired with No 86413 on a timetabled passenger service from Preston. On 12, 15 and 16 August, No 90004 worked the 14.30 Euston-Glasgow, and by October the class was to be seen working a variety of WCML services. Euston's second Class 90 naming took place on 10 October 1988 when HRH the Princess Royal officially named No 90011 *The Chartered Institute of Transport*, a name originally to have been carried by a Class 86.

Modified IC125 Class 43 power cars entered public service between Euston and Birmingham/Wolverhampton in December 1987. Successful trial running resulted in an order for 52 Mk 3 DVTs for WCML services, the first of which began trials in December 1988.

The 'Harlequin Line' brand name was bestowed on the Euston-Watford dc line in 1988, and the Bletchley-based '313' units operating the line were given a new logo. In an endeavour to bring a sparkle to the line, a special 'Gala Day' was organised at Wembley Central. A resignalling scheme to replace the line's 1933-vintage equipment was completed in December 1988 at a cost of £2.5 million.

Above:
**It is 'all change' at Liverpool Street for the passengers who have just arrived from Norwich behind Class 86/2 No 86245 *Dudley Castle*. The station has undergone considerable changes since this 8 May 1987 photograph.**
*Kevin Lane*

Left:
**From 1988, Class 317 EMUs gradually took over the Milton Keynes and Birmingham services from Euston which had previously been in the hands of Class 310 and 312 units. Class 317/1 No 317335, resplendent in Network SouthEast Sector livery, approaches Euston on 7 September 1988 forming the 14.28 from Milton Keynes, and is seen on Camden Bank.** *Brian Morrison*

Below left:
**On 9 September 1988, the 14.30 InterCity service from Euston to Glasgow Central surges away from the London terminus powered by Class 90 No 90004. These locomotives commenced scheduled operation from Euston on a regular basis during the latter part of 1988 — six diagrams being introduced in December.**
*Brian Morrison*

# 3
# New Electrification Schemes

During 1987 and 1988, electrification of Britain's railway system progressed apace, with Network SouthEast being the principal beneficiary. In addition, electrification was completed on the North London line, dispensing with the diesel power that was previously required to haul 'dead' electric locomotives over the non-electrified route linking the WCML with the Norwich main line. Electrification continued on the ECML in preparation for Class 91 working to Edinburgh, and the Bournemouth to Weymouth line, once rumoured for closure, became 'live' in 1988.

## Watford-St Albans Abbey

The 6½-mile branch from Watford-St Albans Abbey was electrified in 1988 and, on 4 July, the 25kV overhead system was energised — the work having cost around £675,000. Traffic had been increasing prior to electrification and, from 11 July, the 'Abbey Flyer' Class 313 EMUs provided a more modern, comfortable service for passengers.

## Royston-Cambridge

On 2 May 1988 through trains were introduced over the newly electrified line from Cambridge to Royston and on to King's Cross using Class 317 EMUs. Electrification of this route has increased efficiency through reduced costs and more efficient rolling stock utilisation.

Left:
**The 12.53 'Abbey Flyer' from Watford to St Albans Abbey arrives at its destination on 18 July 1988, the duty having been allocated to Class 313 EMU No 313002. This line changed to electric operation during the previous week.**
*Brian Morrison*

Below:
**Coming to a scheduled halt at Meldreth station on 22 July 1988, Class 317/1 EMU No 317345 forms the 17.00 Cambridge-King's Cross service. Electric trains operated through services over this route from 2 May 1988.** *Rex Kennedy*

## East Coast Main Line

By the midsummer of 1987, excellent progress was being made on the ECML electrification and the driver instruction classroom three coach EMU had been moved from York to Doncaster in readiness for test running between there and King's Cross. On 7 March 1988, the Peterborough to Grantham section was energised, bringing an electric service to Grantham by the 1988 summer timetable. By 11 April, the current was switched on between Grantham and Leeds (just to a point short of the station) and, at the same time, electrification preparation work was in hand at Edinburgh Waverley, involving the realignment of Platform 10. On 29 September 1988, the first anchor mast was positioned at Waverley and the first wires attached. Back in Yorkshire, the line into Leeds City station was finally energised on 4 July 1988 and test running of electric locomotives was able to begin ahead of schedule.

## North London Link

On 11 November 1987 the first electrically-hauled Railfreight train traversed the newly-electrified WCML/ ECML link, conveying a VIP party. The train ran from Euston to Peterborough hauled by Class 85 No 85011, the first of its class to work on the ECML. The 25kV electrification of this six-mile link has increased the efficiency of locomotive diagramming and utilisation.

Scheduled electric working began on 7 December 1987, but the one through passenger train to use the link, the daytime Glasgow/Edinburgh-Harwich boat train, the 'European', sadly ceased on 16 May. The final northbound 'European' was powered by Class 86/4 No 86404, itself unusual as the train was diagrammed for a Class 86/2.

## London, Tilbury & Southend Re-energised at 25kV

In April 1988, work began on conversion of the 6.25kV overhead electric supply to 25kV from Fenchurch Street station to East Ham car sheds, and from Leigh to Shoeburyness. This will enable the forthcoming 'Networker 2' units to traverse the route in 1991/92.

## East Croydon to East Grinstead

The first electrified passenger services to East Grinstead ran on 26 September 1987, using Class 421 and 423 EMUs. Celebrations took place on the day, and from 5 October 1987 regular electric services ran to and from London. Prior to this, Class 205 and 207 DEMUs had operated services over this route.

**The bridge which overlooks the southern end of Doncaster station was once a favourite haunt for the railway photographer. Sadly, since erection of the catenary masts carrying overhead wires as a result of the ECML electrification, photography is not nearly as popular at this location. Making the best of a bad job, the photographer records Class 56 No 56110 passing the station with a southbound empty MGR train on 18 August 1988.**
*Brian Morrison*


**Electrification of the North London line, which links the East & West Coast main lines, was completed in November 1987. On the 11th of that month, the first electrically-hauled train to traverse the route, conveying a VIP party from Euston to Peterborough, was powered by Class 85 No 85011, hauling two Pullman coaches from the 'Lakeland Pullman' set and a variety of modern freight wagons. It was pictured at Camden Road station in miserable, dull, wet weather.** *Brian Morrison*

## Solent Electrification

On 28 July 1988, in a 'golden pot' ceremony, the Minister of State for Transport, Michael Portillo MP, laid the first conductor rail into its insulating pot to commemorate the start of work on the £16.4 million Solent electrification scheme. The work, covering the lines from Portsmouth to Eastleigh and Southampton, is due for completion by May 1990 and will allow the ageing DEMUs at present employed on the service to be withdrawn. After electrification is completed, Network SouthEast hopes to introduce a through London-Fareham service.

**The 07.20 Harwich Parkeston Quay-Glasgow Central and Edinburgh — the 'European' — ceased to operate from the 1988 Summer timetable. The last 'European' ran on 14 May 1988 hauled by Class 86/4 No 86404, sporting a small 'Last Day' notice in the cab window. This train was normally Class 86/2-powered and prior to electrification of the North London line would have been dragged over this section of line by a Class 47. The train is pictured at Canonbury where the newly electrified tracks have been singled.**
*Brian Morrison*

## Bournemouth to Weymouth

From the start of the 1988 summer passenger timetable, through electric services were running from Waterloo, via Southampton and Bournemouth, to Weymouth, releasing some Class 33/1 diesel locomotives from the push-pull duties on which they had been employed. The first electric train to operate to Weymouth comprised Class 411 4-CEP units Nos 1611/21 on 1 February 1988. However, Class 33/1 No 33106 was attached to the Weymouth end of the train in case of emergency. The electrification scheme was thorough, and provision was even made for the local badgers which habitually crossed the line at certain points, and which would have been electrocuted by the third rail if gaps had not been left adjacent to the badger's known crossing places. This provision has not proved to be completely successful.

Since the line has been energised to Weymouth, a wide variety of EMUs have appeared, including 4-VEPs, 4-CIGs, 4-CEPs and, of course, the new Class 442 'Wessex Electrics'. Perhaps one day we shall see fast Weymouth-Waterloo expresses stopping only at Bournemouth and Southampton — at present they still call at most stations between Bournemouth and Weymouth.

Top:
**Although the headcode '97' displayed on the front of Class 416/3 2-EPB unit No 6327 indicates that the train is on a Lymington Pier service, the location is actually Homerton on the now-electrified North London line, and the train is the 18.35 North Woolwich-Richmond working!** *Brian Morrison*

Above:
**Approaching Southend Central station on 22 October 1988, Class 308 EMU No 308162 forms the 14.42 service from Fenchurch Street to Shoeburyness. This section of the ex-London, Tilbury & Southend Railway route was scheduled to be converted from 6.25kV to 25kV by March 1989.** *Brian Morrison*

Below:
**Class 442 'Wessex Electric' unit No 2406 approaches Moreton with the 12.54 Weymouth-Waterloo on 6 May 1988.** *David Warwick*

# 4
# Focus on Southampton

In recent years, Southampton has proved to be a very interesting location where a variety of motive power and types of traffic can be seen.

During 1988, the Class 442 'Wessex Electrics' made their debut there, although initially some lingered longer than intended due to problems experienced in uncoupling the two units of a 10-car train before the leading set from Waterloo raced on to Bournemouth and Weymouth, to be followed by its partner stopping at all stations to Bournemouth.

Wessex line trains were always a source of interest for the enthusiast at Southampton during 1988 — one never knew whether a train would arrive with one or two Class 73/1s, or even a renumbered example (732xx series) providing the power. Generally, locomotives were marshalled at the London end of the formation, although it was not unknown for a locomotive to be attached to the end of the train. It should also not be forgotten, that a few of the traditional 12-car 4-REP/4-TC formations remained in service during the year. Of particular interest was the variety of temporary EMU formations; indeed on one occasion a 13-coach down express appeared at Southampton comprising 4-REP No 2007 powering a 5-TCB and 4-TC combination! Just to add to the confusion Class 33s also put in appearances on these trains.

Below:
**On 13 May 1988, Class 73/1 No 73111 heads a fast push-pull Weymouth-Waterloo service towards Southampton. The 8-coach train comprises two 4-TC units. It was normal for the locomotive to be positioned at the London end of the train but, on occasions, the motive power appeared at the Bournemouth end.** *David Warwick*

InterCity trains, en route from Poole to Manchester, Birmingham, Liverpool and Edinburgh were usually Class 47-hauled, travelling as far as Basingstoke before leaving the electrified lines to head towards Reading. Class 50s started to appear on Portsmouth to Exeter services during the summer of 1988 — a pleasant sight indeed — and the ever-faithful Class 205 and 207 DEMUs could still be heard chugging their way from Southampton to Fareham, Portsmouth and up to Salisbury.

On the freight scene, Southampton has plenty of variety. With two Freightliner terminals, at Millbrook and Maritime, container trains pass through the station regularly, and in the yards on the east side of Southampton commodities such as cement, timber, bricks and vehicles are conveyed from industrial sites. Businesses with bases in the area include Redland, Blue Circle Cement, Crown

Portland Cement and Butterley Bricks, to name but a few, and the large Ford factory manufacturing Transit vans is situated at nearby Eastleigh.

With Fawley oil refinery being located just west of Southampton, a regular flow of oil trains pass through the station, and there was even a Foster Yeoman stone train, powered by a Class 59 diesel, which reached Eastleigh from the Salisbury direction en route from Merehead to Crawley, in Sussex. A Redland roof tiles depot was officially opened on 13 January 1988 at Eling Wharf, Totton, although it had been in operation since October 1987. It handles a trip working each weekday morning from Eastleigh with tiles from the Redland works at Leighton Buzzard and Clifton, near Rugby. In July 1988, Southampton Maritime Freightliner depot had its contract to move cargo for P&O Containers Ltd and Associated Container Transportation Services Ltd renewed for 16 months, the business being worth £11 million a year. The contract involves the movement of 110 container wagons daily to locations such as Barking, Birmingham, Coatbridge, Leeds, Liverpool and Manchester. During the year ending 31 March 1988, the depot handled 137,000 containers. On 10 October 1988, Freightliner and Railfreight's Speedlink sub-Sector formed a new Railfreight Distribution sub-Sector in an attempt to streamline the movement of freight in Britain, forming a single administration for rail conveyance of export/import cargo. At Southampton Western Docks, Foster Yeoman is to build an aggregates coating plant on Associated British Ports land formerly occupied by railway sidings. Perhaps we shall see more of the Class 59s at Southampton in the not too distant future. Sadly, it was the end for Redbridge Permanent Way (PW) depot early in 1989, the foundry having already been closed in September 1988. The author was there to see the last cast made in the foundry on that memorable day — many of the workers still could not believe that it was the end.

Near Redbridge station, the line from Salisbury joins the electrified main Bournemouth line and, prior to May 1988, the Cardiff-Portsmouth Harbour trains which joined the main line here were hauled by Class 33s, a locomotive class widely used in the area on a variety of workings. The 1988 summer timetable saw Class 155 Sprinters take over this duty, adding yet more traction variety to the area.

**The 11.30 Waterloo-Weymouth express passes Millbrook Freightliner Terminal after leaving Southampton on 13 July 1988 headed by a pair of Class 73/1 locomotives, Nos 73118** *The Romney Hythe & Dymchurch Railway* **and 73134** *Woking Homes 1885-1985.* **On this occasion the train was a nine-coach formation made up of a 4-TC and a 5-TCB.** *Rex Kennedy*

Below left:

**Entering Southampton from the west, and seen at Millbrook on 26 May 1988, the 12.48 Bournemouth-Waterloo fast service is powered by Class 432 4-REP No 2001 hauling two Class 438 4-TCs Nos 8028 and 8029 — the classic Bournemouth line formation prior to the introduction of the Class 442 'Wessex Electrics'.** *Chris Wilson*

Top:

**On 13 July 1988 two Class 442 EMUs, with No 2408 leading, form the 10.53 Weymouth-Waterloo express service seen here approaching Southampton. These units entered service on this route in May 1988.** *Rex Kennedy*

Centre right:

**InterCity Sector Class 47/4 No 47613** *North Star* **passes St Denys on 26 May 1988 hauling the 06.57 Newcastle-Poole. Just two blue and grey-liveried coaches mar an otherwise all-InterCity-liveried formation. The line to Portsmouth can be seen diverging to the right.** *Chris Wilson*

Right:

**The 11.21 Southampton-Portsmouth Harbour train arrives at St Denys on 13 July 1988 formed of Class 207 DEMU No 207017. Class 205 units are also utilised on this route, which is scheduled for electrification.** *Rex Kennedy*

Above:
**Sporting Network SouthEast Sector livery, Class 47/4 No 47573 *The London Standard* passes St Denys on 6 May 1988 with a motley collection of InterCity stock forming the down 'Wessex Scot', the 07.44 Edinburgh-Poole train.** *Brian Knight*

Below left:

**On Sunday 15 May 1988, locomotive-haulage of Cardiff-Portsmouth services ceased, the new order being represented by Class 155 Sprinters. On this last day, Class 33/0 No 33027 *Earl Mountbatten of Burma* is seen coming off the non-electrified Salisbury line and passes over the level crossing to Redbridge Permanent Way depot with the 10.46 Westbury-Portsmouth Harbour working.** *Brian Perryman*

Right:

**Class 50 No 50047 *Swiftsure* hauls the 11.05 Exeter St Davids-Portsmouth Harbour train near Netley, east of Southampton. Later the same day, this locomotive worked a Portsmouth-Waterloo service and failed en route, resulting in its withdrawal from service.** *Nick Bartlett*

Below:

**Hauling the 09.22 Ripple Lane-Southampton Maritime Freightliner, Class 47/0 No 47050, carrying the original style of Railfreight Sector livery, passes through Millbrook station on 26 May 1988. Passing in the opposite direction is another Class 47 locomotive on a train of oil tanks.**
*Chris Wilson*

Above:
On 13 July 1988, a Redland bricks train departs from Bevois Park up yard, between Southampton and St Denys, hauled by Class 47/0 No 47291 *The Port of Felixstowe*. This location also includes terminals for Toleman's vehicle transportation and Rugby and Castle cement. On the down side of the line approximately half-a-mile towards Southampton, at Northam down yard, are freight and grain terminals, and premises for Blue Circle cement and Butterley Bricks. *Rex Kennedy*

Below:
Class 47/3 No 47348 *St Christopher's Railway Home* in original Railfreight Sector livery heads eastwards through Redbridge and approaches Southampton on 13 July 1988 with a train of Esso bogie tankers from Fawley oil refinery. *Rex Kennedy*

Above:

**Redbridge PW depot closed in March 1989 but the foundry made its last casting in September 1988. Continuously-welded rail was manufactured at this location and was transported on special wagons all over the BR network. This view shows sleepered track on bogie bolster wagons and the duty shunter, Class 09 No 09026, beside Redbridge station, stabled prior to the crew returning to work after their lunchbreak.**
*Rex Kennedy*

Centre left:

**A Plasser long-welded rail train passes Millbrook on 27 November 1987 en route from Redbridge to Basingstoke for weekend track relaying work near Micheldever in the care of Class 47/3 No 47328. The locomotive is coupled to the chute wagon from which the train is controlled at the work-site. The second wagon is a self-propelled vehicle, capable of moving the complete loaded train. The vehicle that runs along the train is visible at the rear.**
*Geoff Gillham*

Left:

**On 5 November 1988, Class 155 Sprinter No 155319 leaves Southampton forming the 12.10 Portsmouth Harbour-Cardiff Central.** *Brian Morrison*

# 5
# Sprinters, Skippers and Pacers

The Provincial Sector's Class 155 and 156 Super Sprinters operate over a vast network of routes and can now be seen on all regions of BR. As was the case in the Southampton area, these units did not enter full public service on many routes until the 1988 summer timetable and, at the end of 1988, some areas of Britain still awaited their first Sprinters on scheduled services.

## South Wales

The Class 150/2 Sprinters entered service in South Wales from 5 October 1987, operating to Fishguard and Milford Haven. Even the Haverfordwest to London HST service was rediagrammed to start from Swansea with a Class 150/2 Sprinter connection, and provision was already being made for Class 155 Sprinters to operate Haverfordwest to Manchester through trains.

Since May 1987, Cardiff's allocation of Class 150/2 Sprinters had been steadily increasing until, by the start of that year's winter timetable on 5 October, the majority of services calling at Central and Queen Street stations were Sprinter workings. The improved performance and availability of the new units, compared with the conventional DMUs that they replaced, allowed a major recast of valley lines services — indeed, Cardiff enjoyed an increase of 131 trains a day! Nevertheless, some local services remained in the hands of the familiar Class 101, 116 and 117 DMUs.

With the advent of Sprinters in South Wales, new stations in the Cardiff area were already being envisaged, together with the operation of trains from Tondu and Bridgend to Cardiff, and the reopening of the Aberdare line to passengers. The latter project came to fruition in October 1988, the service being operated by Class 150/2 Sprinters, and six new stations were opened on the route. Trains ran every 2hr (hourly on Saturdays) and it is hoped to improve the service should traffic levels justify this.

From May 1988, Cardiff Central became a beneficiary of the new 'Provincial Express' service, which included routes to Brighton, Portsmouth, Liverpool, Weston-super-Mare, Birmingham, Gloucester, Manchester, Weymouth and Holyhead, to name but a few.

## North Wales

On 24 February 1988, a two-car Class 155 unit, No 155314, made its inaugural trip on the North Wales coast line from Crewe to Holyhead and, on 17 May, a re-formed three-car Class 150/1 Sprinter, No 150141, worked a Bangor to Chester service. Its centre

Below:
**Inside BREL York works on 2 September 1987, the penultimate unit of the Class 150/2 fleet, No 150284, nears completion and awaits one lighting cluster and the remainder of its 'Sprinter' transfers. After being outshopped, this unit was allocated to Haymarket depot.** *Brian Morrison*

car, sporting a later version of Provincial Sector livery than the other two, was No 57253, from unit No 150253. Testing was carried out on 17 July on the Conwy Valley branch with Class 150/1 Sprinter No 150122 to see if these units could overcome the problem of excessive wheelflange squealing over sharp curves in an endeavour to get the ban on using Sprinters on this branch lifted. Some Plymouth Laira-based Class 142 railbuses were transferred to Newton Heath, Manchester, in October 1987, and the chocolate and cream-liveried No 142023 made its North Wales service debut on the Llandudno branch on 6 November. This attractive GWR-style livery makes these units look rather special. Holyhead was the scene of a derailed Class 142 Skipper, No 142018, in January 1988.

## The West Country

From October 1987, Class 142 Skipper railbuses were transferred from Plymouth Laira to Newton Heath and Neville Hill following unsatisfactory performance on many West Country routes, and Class 108 units supplemented the indigenous DMU fleet in replacing the new units. By May 1988, Class 155 Sprinters had percolated west, and were working to Taunton, Exeter, Paignton and Penzance.

The top photo shows a Class 150/1 Sprinter at Frodsham station.





Above:
**On 6 October 1988 the long-distance 12.50 Bangor-Hull Sprinter service leaves Frodsham following its timetabled stop. The unit is a York-built Class 150/1, No 150130, which will take 4½hr for the complete journey, and is scheduled to arrive at Hull at 17.18.** *Brian Morrison*

Right:
**A purpose-built track recording train (comprising car Nos DB999600/01) stands at Paddington station on 2 November 1987, when it was officially handed over by the manufacturers to representatives of Derby RTC. The bodyshell of a Class 150/1 Sprinter was used to house the onboard technical equipment.** *Brian Morrison*

## The Northwest

Manchester first saw the chocolate and cream Class 142 Skippers in the summer of 1987. These units supplemented the already large fleet of Class 142 units at Newton Heath, and certain services, such as the Manchester Victoria to Rochdale 'loop', were almost exclusively Class 142-operated. Gearbox problems developed on the class during 1987 and, in July of that year, only 31 of the 57 Newton Heath-allocated Pacers were available for service owing to transmission problems. By February 1988 10 units could be seen stored at Crewe Carriage Shed awaiting replacement gearboxes.

Although Class 150 Sprinters allocated to Newton Heath had operated in the northwest for some time, from the commencement of the 1988 summer timetable Class 155-operated services to and from the northwest included trains from Liverpool, Manchester and Crewe to Cardiff and Swansea, crew training having started at Longsight in February and at Chester in April.

Class 156 Super Sprinters also entered service in 1988. These appeared on trains from Manchester, Liverpool and Blackpool to Cambridge, Norwich, Lowestoft, Yarmouth, Ipswich, Harwich (Parkeston Quay) and Nottingham.

## The Midlands and East Anglia

The Class 150/1 Sprinters have been allocated to Derby Etches Park since their introduction and are used on services to destinations such as Birmingham and Crewe, but lack of capacity meant that by June 1988 five units had been strengthened to three-car formations by including a centre car taken from disbanded Class 150/2s.

From 11 July 1988, the Swindon-Gloucester-Cheltenham service was worked by Class 150 units drafted in from Manchester and, on 25 July, Sprinters Nos 150120/135 formed the first Ironbridge Gorge passenger ser-

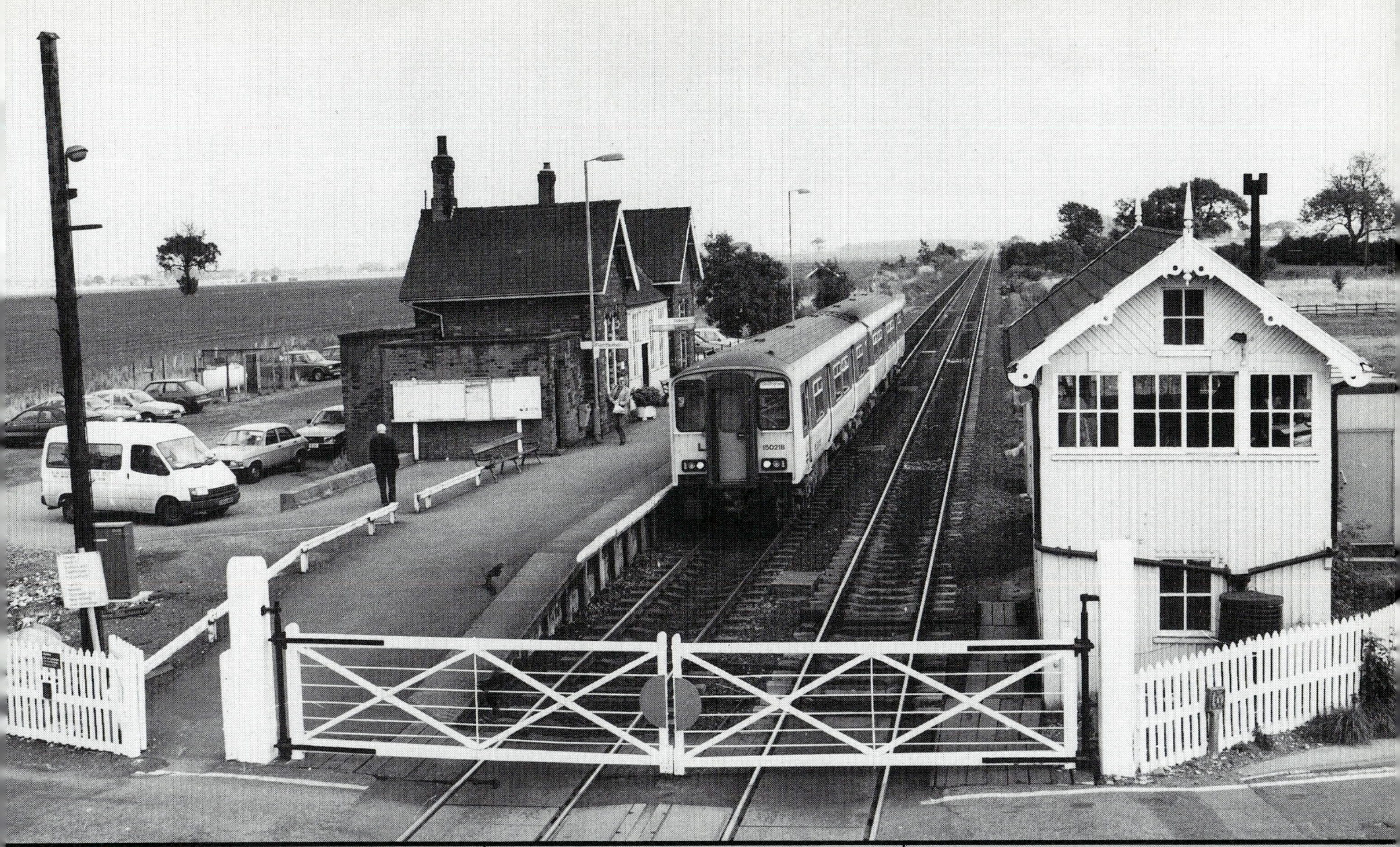

Above:
**Forming the 14.00 Barton-on-Humber-Cleethorpes service on 25 September 1987, Class 150/2 Sprinter No 150218 makes the scheduled stop at Habrough station.** *Brian Morrison*

vice of the summer. The 1988 timetable saw Class 155 Sprinters operating from Birmingham, Worcester and Gloucester to Cardiff; from Oxford to Worcester, Hereford and Bristol, and from Crewe to Shrewsbury and Craven Arms. The '155s' had been operating Worcester-Hereford trains since 21 March.

Leamington Spa was the starting place for the special train, comprising unit No 155304, conveying invited guests to the reopening of Birmingham Snow Hill station on 2 October 1987. On the same day, Leamington also saw Class 155 Sprinter No 155306, attached to chocolate and cream-liveried Class 142 unit No 142025, passing through whilst undergoing special gauging tests organised by the Derby RTC. This test was carried out to ensure that there would be no coupling problems during multiple operation of these two classes before the '155s' were delivered to West Yorkshire.

During February 1988, trials were carried out using Class 156 Super Sprinter No 156401 on the Derby to Leicester route, testing continuing at Bristol in March, but before that, in January, Norwich had received No 156402 for crew training, prior to the class eventually taking over Norwich to Birmingham services from the Class 31/4 and Mk 2 stock formations previously employed. Nos 156403/4/5 were employed for crew training at Newton Heath, Derby and Tyseley and No 156406 was used between Norwich and Peterborough. However, deliveries of the class were slow, and Norwich to Birmingham trains had to be operated by Class 150/1 units as a temporary measure until 11 July. By late July, Norwich-allocated Class 156s were working in abundance throughout East Anglia and the East Midlands, 19 diagrams having operated from Norwich since 20 June.

By September 1988, Class 156 deliveries were really stepping up. However, rectification of minor faults was necessary and conventional DMUs (Tyseley-based), including Classes 101, 108, 115, 116, 117 and 118, were substituted on certain Midland duties.

Below:
**A six-car excursion train from the Wirral, comprising Class 155 unit No 155310 (leading) and Class 156 units Nos 156401/403, traverses the WCML at Winwick, near Warrington, on 30 April 1988. For recognition purposes, the two types have differing roof panels.**
*Les Nixon*

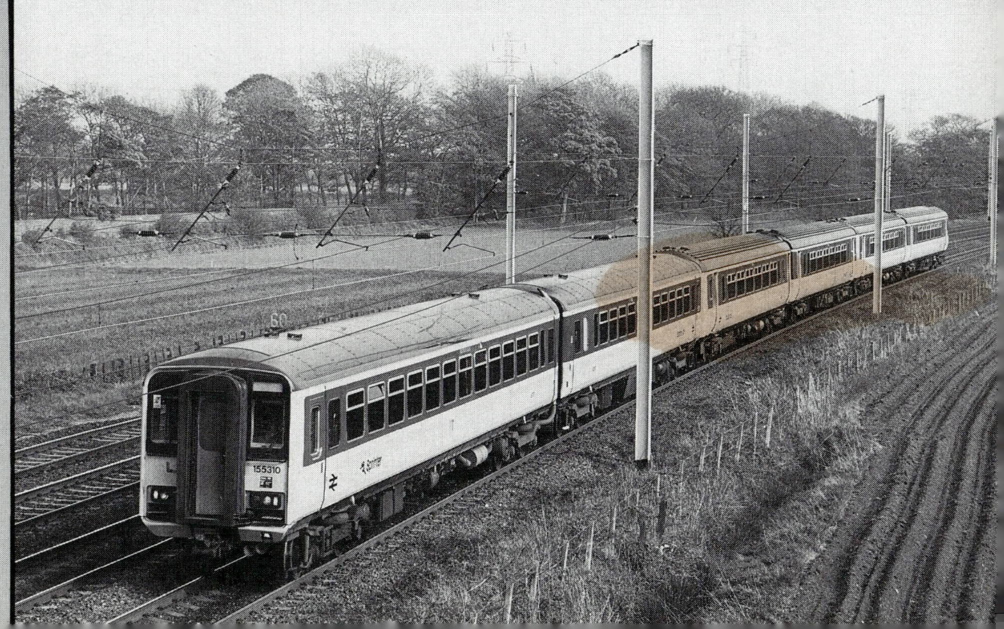

## Scotland

Prior to the introduction of Class 150/2 Sprinters on Dundee services, the Tay Bridge centenary on 20 June 1987 was celebrated by the use of No 150257 on a special shuttle service over the bridge, but on Edinburgh to Bathgate services, criticism was voiced over the use of these two-car units at peak periods due to their limited seating accommodation. However, since the introduction of the Class 150s on services from Edinburgh to Dundee and Bathgate in October 1987, punctuality had vastly improved, and usage was up by 4%.

The Class 156 Super Sprinters reached Scotland for the first time in 1988, when No 156402 completed various journeys during the week ending 24 January. It reached Kyle of Lochalsh, Fort William, Mallaig and Oban as well as working around Glasgow, Dundee and Aberdeen in preparation for the takeover of services to these areas from the start of the 1988 winter timetable.

In July 1988, No 156424 was dispatched from Norwich to Edinburgh Haymarket for the training of crews and maintenance staff prior to the '156s' taking up diagrams on the G&SW route to Stranraer from October. These trains are based at Corkerhill depot and heavy maintenance work will be carried out at Haymarket. For West Highland lines

Top left:

**A Class 141 Leyland Railbus, comprising cars Nos 55504/24, displays its old West Yorkshire PTE green and cream colours at York station on 2 September 1988 waiting to operate a Harrogate service.** *Brian Morrison*

Centre left:

**Class 143 Alexander Barclay Pacers Nos 143020 and 143021 leave Battersby on 23 April 1988 forming the 16.05 Whitby-Middlesbrough service. The yellow and white livery with blue waistband signifies ownership by the Tyne & Wear PTE.** *David Masterman*

Left:

**On 24 October 1987, Class 144 Pacer No 144009 leaves Bingley with the 11.06 (SO) Skipton-Leeds service, painted in the new West Yorkshire PTE colours of red and cream. In March 1988, BREL Derby delivered intermediate coaches for the '144s' (see centre right illustration) to provide longer trains for the Leeds-Ilkley and Leeds-York services which have been experiencing some overcrowding.** *John Oxley*

Right:
**Class 156 Sprinter No 156414 passes New Mills South Junction on 17 August 1988 forming the rather unlikely 15.35 service from Liverpool Lime Street to Lowestoft. The train makes scheduled stops at Warrington Central, Birchwood, Manchester Oxford Road and Piccadilly, Stockport, Chesterfield, Derby, Nottingham, Grantham, Peterborough, Ely, Thetford and Norwich, before it finally arrives at its destination at 21.47; a journey time of over 6hr.** *Brian Morrison*

Below:
**The 14.05 Morecambe-Leeds train on 4 June 1988 comprised one three-car and one two-car Class 144 units. This formation, with No 144020 leading, is pictured passing through the scenic countryside at Bell Busk.** *Bill Sharman*

duties, Six Class 156 units have been fitted with Radio Electronic Token Block equipment, and the first unit to arrive at Inverness for train crew familiarisation was No 156445, in October 1988.

Introduction of Class 156s has prompted Provincial in Scotland to pursue further the practice of bestowing names on their principal services. The 13.09 Newcastle-Stranraer became the 'Galloway Enterprise', the 17.15 Newcastle-Girvan, 'The Ayrshire Trader', the 07.00 Girvan-Newcastle, 'The Tyne Trader', and the 11.05 Stranraer-Newcastle, 'The Tyne Enterprise'. Both the 08.23 Newcastle-Glasgow and the corresponding return working are named 'The Borderer'.

## The Northeast

The 25 Class 143 Pacers, allocated to Heaton depot, were plagued with gearbox problems throughout the period under review. Many of these units carry the Tyne & Wear PTE yellow, white and blue livery and carry the 'TW Pacer' logo. Voith gearboxes have replaced the Self Changing Gears (SCG) boxes on all Class 143 units.

Left:
**A scene at Crewe Carriage Shed on 12 February 1988 when Class 142 Pacers could be found stored and awaiting new gearboxes. Heading this line of dormant units is No 142045, and others in store at this date included Nos 142002/007/008/010/029/032/045.** *Brian Morrison*

Throughout 1987 and 1988 poor Class 143 availability meant that a number of diagrams in the Northeast were worked by traditional DMUs, often in a poor state of repair, and locomotive-hauled sets powered by Class 47/4s (including those with long-range fuel tanks) and Class 31s.

By March 1988 many of the Class 143s had returned to traffic and shortly afterwards Heaton received a Class 142 Pacer (No 142050), with a Voith gearbox, for crew familiarisation. Three of this class were allocated to Heaton in July to cover for those Class 143s being fitted with Voith gearboxes, a job being undertaken at RFS Engineering, Doncaster. By midsummer 1988, the units were permitted to operate on the Wear Valley line.

## Yorkshire

Neville Hill depot, Leeds, has an allocation of Class 141, 142, and 144 railbuses — including some chocolate and cream-liveried Class 142s received during 1987 — in addition to Class 150/2 and 155 Sprinters for trans-Pennine duties. The Class 144s were delivered in the attractive West Yorkshire red and cream livery and were put to work on a variety of local services, widening their sphere of operation to include the Huddersfield-Sheffield services from the summer of 1987. Unfortunately these units, despite being a later design, also suffered from problems with their gearboxes and wheelsets. Five sets received Voith equipment at BREL Derby as the SCG gearboxes were

fitted to 10 new centre cars to form three-car units. This was to alleviate overcrowding on some peak-hour services, and these were delivered in March 1988, being used on Leeds-Ilkley and Leeds-York via Harrogate services. Later in the year, in June, the first of West Yorkshire's original Class 141 railbuses to be refurbished, No 141109, was returned from Andrew Barclay of Kilmarnock. The revamped units include a neater front end with standardised automatic couplers to enable multiple operation with all Pacer and Sprinter classes. In July, all Neville Hill-based Class 150/2s had three seats removed from the DMS(L) vehicle to provide passenger luggage facilities, following complaints of insufficient capacity on trans-Pennine services, and on the 28th of that month the first of seven Class 155/1 units, No 155341, was delivered to the depot.

Crew training on the '155' took place at Holbeck, and on 3 August it was joined by Class 156 unit No 156432. On 16 August, No 155342, looking resplendent in its red and cream livery, carried out tests between Carlisle and Carstairs prior to entering service with its six contemporaries on 'Calder Valley' York-Preston duties.

Doncaster Major Depot undertook maintenance and repair work on Sprinters during 1988. April saw the start of a programme of bogie changes on Class 150/1s — a feat often achieved almost overnight — and June saw the first Class 156 to visit Doncaster, No 156410, for collision repairs, to be followed by its first Class 155, No 155306, for the same reason the following month.

The Provincial revolution had reached Yorkshire with a vengeance!

Above left:
**The location is Wigan Wallgate station, where Class 142/1 Pacer No 142054 is seen forming the 10.30 Manchester Victoria-Kirkby via Atherton train on 27 June 1988. In the background is the 10.40 Manchester Victoria-Southport via Bolton connecting service, formed of Class 150/2 Sprinter No 150217.**
*John Glover*

Left:
**A reminder of when the Class 142 Skippers were operating in the West Country with unit No 142018, in its chocolate and cream livery, seen approaching Crediton as the 12.33 Barnstaple-Exmouth service. The old L&SWR signalbox dates from 1875.**
*Brian Morrison*

Left:

**The orange and brown livery of the Greater Manchester PTE is depicted here on Class 142 Pacer No 142013 seen leaving Platform 11 at Manchester Victoria station — at one time the longest platform in the United Kingdom when it continued on into Manchester Exchange. The train is the 17.37 to Southport.** *John Glover*

Below:

**The first of seven Class 155/1 Sprinters to receive West Yorkshire PTE red and cream livery, No 155341, enters Leeds on 12 September 1988 for its inaugural run to York, conveying invited guests.** *Ian S. Carr*

# 6
# Yorkshire Relish

Yorkshire has always offered plenty to interest the railway enthusiast over the years, and locations such as Doncaster, York and Leeds have always featured a variety of traction.

Electrification of the ECML has progressed into Yorkshire and even Leeds now sees electric trains. Pacer and Sprinter liveries compete with the colourful Railfreight liveries carried by locomotives emanating from Tinsley, and the Class 319 and 321 units turned out from York Works in Network SouthEast livery add to the variety. More and more stations are opening in Yorkshire today — gone are the days when closure was the norm.

During 1987, three new stations opened on the West Yorkshire 'Metro' system: East Garforth, Frizinghall and Sandal & Agbrigg. Eleven new stations are scheduled to open in the county by 1992, and others proposed include Walsden in Calderdale, Armley and Milnsbridge, on the outskirts of Huddersfield, the aim being to cater for the inhabitants of densely-populated areas. In Bradford, Forster Square station gained some InterCity services in October 1988, taking over from Bradford Interchange. The town of Shipley, a rapidly-developing centre, is therefore now served by InterCity trains and a 'park-and-ride' scheme there attracts custom from North Bradford, Airedale and Wharfedale.

Below:
**The triangular station at Shipley has always been an interesting location for railway photographers. On 7 May 1988, one of the three-car Class 144 Pacers, No 144018, forming a train to Morecambe, passes the station's 1907 Midland Railway signalbox.**
*D. Stuart Lindsey*

Unfortunately one station did actually close during 1988: Rowntree Halt in York, which saw its last passenger service on 8 July, freight traffic on the short branch ceasing shortly afterwards.

In July 1988, a proposal was made to divert Leeds to Barnsley/Sheffield trains through Castleford which would result in the closure of Altofts station and the withdrawal of passenger services between Methley Junction and Altofts Junction. This re-routeing would allow Provincial to offer an improved service on the Leeds to Castleford line, and would provide a new link from Castleford to Wakefield, Barnsley and Sheffield.

From 6 June 1988, one extra first-class coach was added to the formation of the 'Yorkshire Pullman', increasing first-class accommodation from 185 seats to 233. There are also 207 standard-class seats on this train, the 07.15 Leeds-King's Cross. It

returns from London at 17.50. The success of the Pullman service has led to a 40% growth in the number of first-class passengers using this train.

In South Yorkshire, railway development has been limited, owing to the very low bus fares in the county, but Rotherham Central station has been reopened and is served by Sheffield to Doncaster local services and the two-hourly Sprinter service from Nottingham to Leeds, via Sheffield. Since 16 May 1988, a new hourly service to Sheffield has operated from Leeds, running via Rotherham Central, Moorthorpe and two new stations at Thurnscoe and Goldthorpe. Various plans are afoot to reopen more stations in South Yorkshire by May 1991.

Tinsley depot in South Yorkshire was the last home for the Class 45

Right:
**A typically busy scene south of York station on 28 May 1988 showing three varied passenger workings. On the right is the 07.00 Glasgow Queen Street-Newquay HST, led by HST power car No 43166, and in the centre of the picture Class 142 Pacer No 142086, in Provincial Sector blue livery, changes platforms after arrival from Leeds in order to form a return service. In the background Class 47/4 No 47664 awaits departure with the 11.20 York-Cardiff Central train.** *Brian Morrison*

Left:
**Following completion of electrification of the main line into Leeds station, the first electrically-powered train was a test working on 11 August 1988 hauled by Class 91 No 91004. At Leeds it has only proved necessary to provide facilities for electric trains at Platforms 5, 6 and 8 and at the east end of Platform 4.** *Alan Whitaker*

Below left:
**BREL Doncaster's wagon works was taken over by RFS Industries Ltd in October 1987, and the new organisation continued the BREL contract with English China Clays for new CDA china clay wagons. Later the company also won the contract for fitting Voith gearboxes to Tyneside Pacers. The chequered yellow and blue shunter *Terence*, belonging to RFS Industries Ltd, is seen outside the works.**
*David Ware*

'Peaks' on revenue-earning duty, and they will be sadly missed. The depot was also responsible for affixing names to the last serviceable members of the class. A total of eight Class 45/0s, 12 Class 45/1s, and five Departmental Class 97s ended their days at Tinsley during 1988.

## Electrification

The electrification into Leeds was heralded on 11 August 1988 by Class 91 No 91004 entering the station on a test train over a year ahead of the originally planned full-service date of October 1989. At Doncaster, the large bridge which spans the track south of the station proved a bit of a headache at first as clearances for overhead wires were expected to necessitate lowering the track. However, the York Project Manager's scheme to overcome this problem saved around £1.5 million. As the other spans of the bridge were occupied by only one track, it proved possible to construct huge buttresses which not only supported the other arches of this five-span bridge, unaltered, but would also support a concrete beam structure to give the necessary clearance for the four centre tracks. Further north, at Wakefield Westgate, the up through line was removed as surplus to requirements — indeed, the electrification planners would have liked to have seen the down through line go as well, but this was not practicable. Owing to operational considerations on the approaches to Leeds, it was not considered necessary to electrify both routes from Wakefield, and the decision was therefore taken to close the slower and more expensive-to-maintain 'Viaduct Line'. This allowed train timings between Leeds and Wakefield to be reduced by 4min. Nevertheless, the 'Viaduct Line' formation is at present being retained pending West Yorkshire PTE's planned expansion of services, which could require the reopening of the line. Reopening would, however, require the electrification masts serving the headshunt at the Leeds end of

Above:
**Inside the premises of what is now BRML Doncaster, Classes 56, 47, 37 and 31 receive attention on 17 November 1988. The actual locomotives which can be seen in this view are Nos 56063, 47607 *Royal Worcester*, 37080 and 31466.** *Brian Morrison*

Left:
**Inside the Paint Shop at BREL York Works on 15 September 1988, the third Class 321 production unit, No 321303, nears completion. The first batch of these units to be constructed is intended for use on the ex-Great Eastern line from Liverpool Street to Shenfield.** *Brian Morrison*

the 'Viaduct Line' to be moved from the centre to the outside of the viaduct.

It has not been necessary to 'wire' Leeds City station in its entirety — only Platforms 5, 6, 8 and the east end of Platform 4 — but at Doncaster all platform lines and through goods lines have been electrified. Beyond Leeds, the wiring extends only as far as Marsh Lane, to provide a head-shunt, but electrification will be extended to Neville Hill depot for ecs movements.

## Doncaster Works

On 11 February 1987, probably the last locomotive to be built at Doncaster Works, Class 58 No 58050, resplendent in Railfreight grey livery, posed beside Class A4 Gresley Pacific No 4498 *Sir Nigel Gresley*, which was constructed at Doncaster exactly 50 years before. No 58050 was equipped with separately-excited (SEPEX) traction motors which provide improved adhesion when starting with a heavy load, and provides precisely the correct amount of electrical current to individual motors. This equipment has been built into the Class 89 and 90 electrics and will also be installed in the new Class 60 diesel. In October



1987, Doncaster Wagon Works became RFS Engineering when RFS Industries Ltd (formed by a team of former BR managers) purchased the works from BR. The company inherited existing contracts for new china clay wagons, and wagon and wheel overhaul. They also became responsible for the fitting of new Voith gearboxes to Class 142 and 143 Pacers.

During the latter months of 1987, the RFS wagon works started to turn out new hopper wagons, designated CDA, for English China Clays, but the first batch developed door mechanism problems and had to be returned to Doncaster. Also around this time, FPA container flats started to appear from RFS's Doncaster works modified from VCAs. RFS Engineering was also responsible for the new batch of ZDV 'Tope' wagons converted from 21-ton HTV coal hoppers. A colourful sight at this location is *Terence*, ex-BR Class 08 shunter No 08331, in its blue, yellow and grey chequered livery.

In April 1987 the BRB's plans to divide its BREL workshops subsidiary were implemented. Doncaster, along with Eastleigh and Glasgow Spring-burn, were detailed to concentrate on Cost Effective Maintenance overhauls: mainly by component exchange, forming a new company, British Rail Maintenance Ltd. The remaining workshops were to continue under the BREL banner for new construction and major rebuilding contracts with a view to becoming a totally independent company.

During 1988, Doncaster Major Depot continued to be responsible for work on Class 08 shunters, Class 20s, 31s, 37s, 47s, 56s, 58s and multiple-units, including CEM exams and collision damage repairs. An interesting visitor was Class 47/9 No 47901, which was repainted in

Above:
**With coal empties from Healey Mills for Grimethorpe Colliery, Departmental Class 97 'Peak' No 97412 pulls away from Calder Bridge Junction, Wakefield, on 22 December 1987.**
*Les Nixon*

Railfreight Construction sub-Sector livery following an 'F' examination in January 1988. The first Class 119 DMU to appear in Network SouthEast livery (Reading-based car No 51079) was outshopped from Doncaster in July 1988.

## York Works

On 2 September 1987, BREL York Works handed over the first of the 60 four-car Class 319 'Thameslink' units, No 319002, to Chris Green, Sector Director, Network SouthEast. The first unit to be outshopped, No 319001, had been extensively fitted out for detailed testing, and on 4 September it was delivered to Strawberry Hill depot from the Derby RTC. The '319s' are equipped for both 25kV overhead current collection and 750V dc third rail, allowing them to be used on both the LMR and SR.

Also in September, BR ordered 46 four-car Class 321 EMUs for Network SouthEast to be built by BREL York for work on the Liverpool Street-Cambridge and Southend Victoria services, allowing existing stock to be withdrawn or cascaded to other lines. The first of these EMUs was rolled out at York Works on 15 September 1988, only 12 months after the order had been placed.

## Freight

October 1987 saw freight locomotives take on a new look with the launch of a new Railfreight livery. Symbols were applied to locomotives to acknowledge their dedication to particular sub-Sectors.

On 27 June 1988, a new main line siding to the Plasmor plant from the ECML was opened at Heck on the West/North Yorkshire border. Previously, concrete blocks were forwarded to Knottingly depot and, prior to 1986, all deliveries were made by road. Increased production necessitated the use of a new siding which means direct delivery by rail from Heck to London and southern depots.

Tinsley depot in South Yorkshire provides the majority of BR's freight motive power, and Tinsley locomotives continued to be seen far and wide, particularly on Speedlink workings. Despite the moves towards sub-Sector dedication of locomotives that had been taking place since 1988, locomotives continued to be found working trains for which their sub-Sector dedications did not apply, control offices preferring to roster incorrect motive power rather than leave services stranded.

# 7
# '88 Freight

The most important news concerning the Railfreight Sector during 1987 was the public launch of a new 'house style', which included the new livery referred to in a previous chapter together with symbols which gave a visual identity to the sub-Sectors. Depot plaques were also applied to locomotives in an attempt to boost morale at depots.

Also of significance has been the many namings of freight locomotives, both after customers using Railfreight services and after locations served.

A ceremony took place on 14 May 1987 when Class 47/0 locomotive No 47016 was named *The Toleman Group* by Dianne Toleman, wife of the company's chairman, at Dagenham Dock. Toleman has operated Ford Motor Co trains from Dagenham Dock and Halewood to distribution depots in Scotland and the Northeast since 1963, using bogie carflats. The prototype 'Procor 80' wagon was unveiled in March 1981 and is still in traffic with Toleman today. The vehicles have been fitted with mesh side-screens to protect cars from vandals.

In November 1987, construction commenced on a new marshalling yard at Margam. The Knuckle Yard, as it is known, comprises 18 sidings with 11 lines having direct access to the nearby British Steel (BSC) complex. The yard occupies a 20-acre site and about 85 trains weekly, carrying an annual total of 70 million tonnes of steel, leave the BSC complex for the yard prior to departing for BSC's other plants in Britain. Coal and lime trains also use the yard, with trains entering from both east and west. The Knuckle Yard replaces the old Margam Hump Yard which became uneconomic to operate.

On 25 November 1987, the double-headed afternoon 'Clayliner' from St Blazey to Gloucester, hauled by Class 37/5 locomotives Nos 37670 and 37671 *Tre Pol and Pen*, ran into a dead-end siding at Tavistock Junction, pushing a Lowmac wagon through the buffers, and consequently both locomotives suffered extensive damage. After being towed back to Laira, the two Class 37s were sent to Crewe Works for repair. Another accident occurred, this time at Cupar in Scotland, on 2 June 1988, when a cement train tore up some 1,000yd of track and destroyed a road bridge. The recovery train was powered by Class 26 No 26014 and it took over a week to repair the track, resulting in Dundee to Ladybank passenger services having to run via Perth, and on to the single line from Hilton Junction to Ladybank via Newburgh.

Copyhold Junction, near Haywards Heath, Sussex, was the scene of an incident on 14 June 1988, when

Below:

**The new Redland Aggregate Terminal at Langley Junction opened in May 1988 with two workings per week from Mountsorrel. This brought Class 56 locomotives to the area for the first time. However, on 19 August 1988, the Class 56, No 56059, allocated to work the 08.30 Redland stone train from Mountsorrel to Radlett had failed and required the assistance of one of the last Class 45/1 'Peaks' No 45115 *Apollo*. This unusual combination is seen leaving Harpenden running 5hr late.**
*John C. Baker*

Right:
**Train 6H45, the 11.47 Oakley-Tunstead empty hoppers, passes Peak Forest on 17 August 1988 headed by Class 47/4 No 47446. Approaching from the opposite direction is a pair of Class 37/5s, Nos 37685 and 37681, powering the 6J46 14.23 Peak Forest-Hope Street consisting of new-style hopper wagons.** *Brian Morrison*

Class 56 No 56062 was derailed and fell down an embankment — the first stage of recovery not being effected until 4 September. At the time of the accident No 56062 had been hauling an Ardingly to Westbury ARC empty stone train. BRML Doncaster won the contract to repair the locomotive in a relatively short time.

Another 'company' naming took place on 3 March 1988, when No 47319 was named *Norsk Hydro* at that company's Immingham works. The company operates fertiliser trains to Leith and Avonmouth and its trains were expected to convey about 350,000 tonnes during 1988 in specially-designed bogie wagons each capable of carrying 58 tonnes.

Scottish freight was often in the news, and on 17 March 1988, the Mauchline to Annbank line in the Nith Valley reopened to traffic. Coal trains (usually hauled by double-headed Class 20s or a single Class 37) are now using this route from Knockshinnock Colliery to Ayr Harbour saving valuable time compared with the old route via Kilmarnock and Barassie. Also in Scotland, adjacent to the Kilmarnock to Barassie line, is a new paper mill at Meadowhead, where sidings have been constructed to allow the movement of raw materials to and from the plant. Railfreight has secured a 10-year contract to move 100,000 tonnes of china clay slurry from Cornwall annually, and 100,000 tonnes of timber from Arrochar, Taynuilt and Fort William.

On 18 May 1988, Class 37/4 locomotive No 373423 was named *Sir Murray Morrison* at the Lochaber smelter in Fort William to commemorate the signing of a new 10-year contract between Railfreight and British Alcan to transport an annual total of 100,000 tonnes of alumina from Blyth, in Northumberland, to the

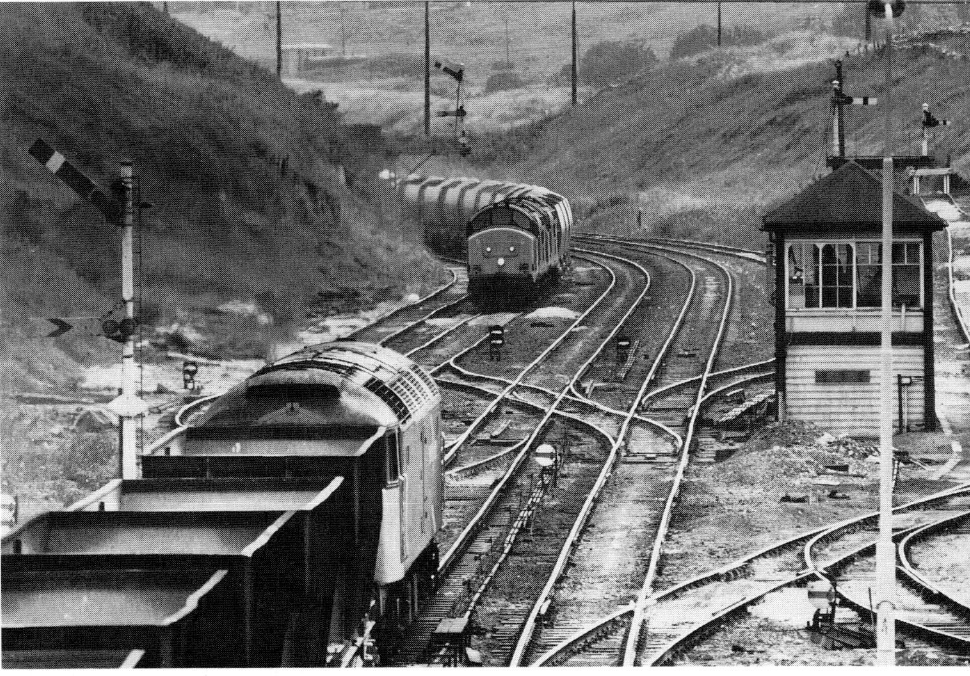

Below:
**Passing the North Staffordshire Railway Society's preserved station at Cheddleton on 30 August 1988, Class 20s Nos 20132 and 20020 head the last British Industrial Sand train to Oakamoor.** *Brian Morrison*

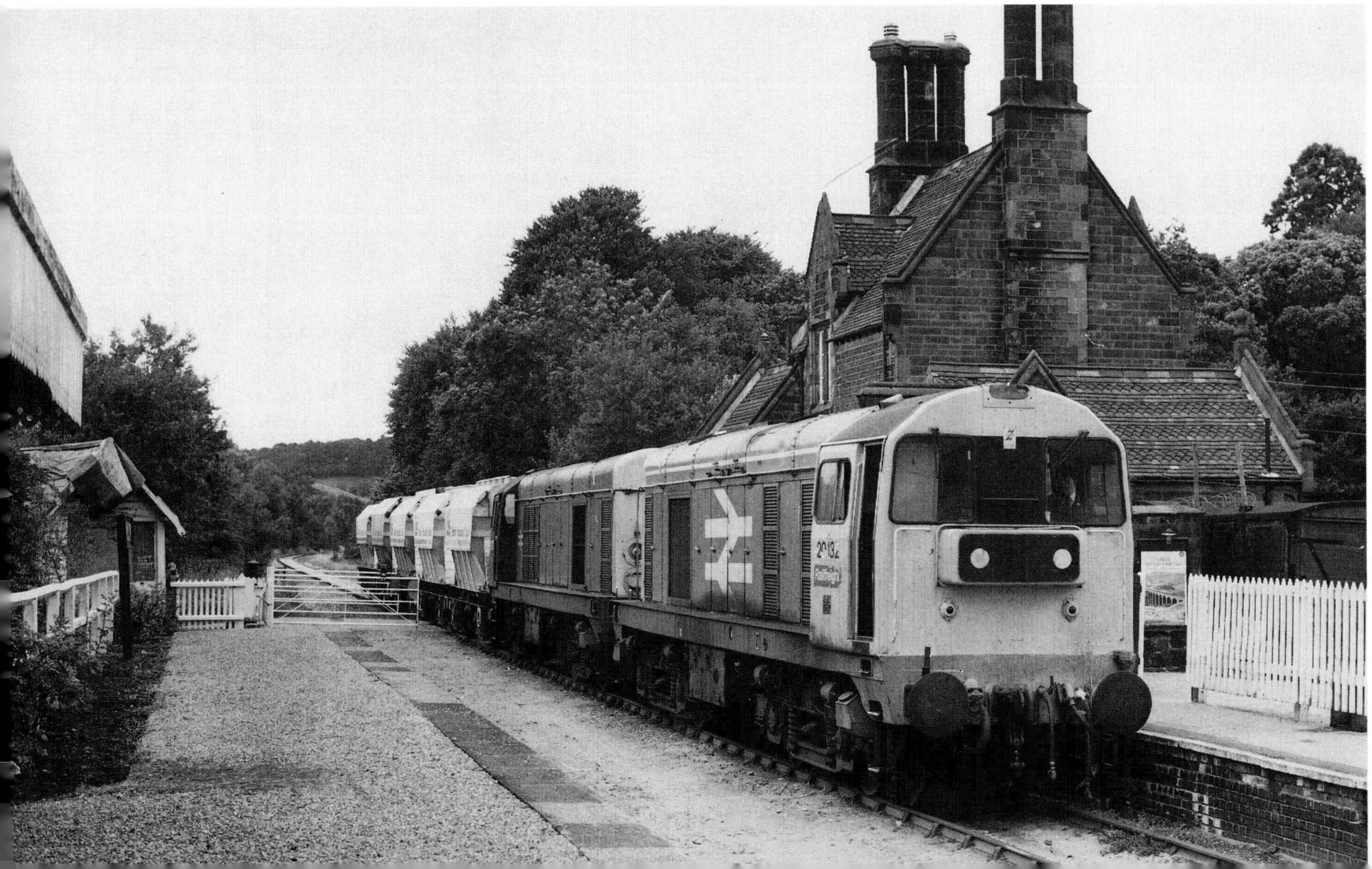

smelters at Lochaber and Kinloch-leven. This comes as a boost for the West Highland line and keeps around 30 lorryloads a day off the local road system, something that should please the holidaymakers. Forty-three new 45-tonne wagons were ordered by British Alcan, running as 13-wagon trains grossing 585 tonnes. These new contracts make the future for the West Highland line look most promising.

A further 1988 naming, on 11 September, was Class 47/0 No 47283 *Johnny Walker*, named after the famous whisky in a ceremony held at Kilmarnock open day.

The 'mothballed' line serving Kincardine power station came back into operation on 4 July 1988. This stretch of line from Longannet power station, and the short stretch between Yoker and Rothesay Dock (Clydebank), was reopened to handle cheap coal from America, China and Australia which is landed at Rothesay Dock for power station use. Railfreight operates two trips daily, generally powered by double-headed Class 20s or Class 26s. Initially HEA wagons were being used on these trains, in rakes of 27, but later HAA wagons were introduced.

Coatbridge Freightliner Terminal, Gartsherrie, saw the introduction of a 'next day' Freightliner service which commenced on 3 October 1988 — this

Right:
**On 10 September 1988, a Weaste-Stanlow train of empty oil tanks passes Deal St Junction on the approaches to Manchester Victoria where it will reverse in order to complete the journey. One of the Class 47/0 locomotives dedicated to Shell Oil traffic, No 47194 *Bullidae*, provides the motive power and shows the latest style of Railfreight Sector livery with Petroleum sub-Sector markings. *Bullidae* is the Latin name of a variety of shell and all the dedicated fleet are named in this fashion.** *Les Nixon*

Below:
**Two Class 37/0 locomotives, with No 37002 leading, and sporting revised Railfreight Sector livery with red solebars, pass the 1916 Great Central Railway signalbox at Wrawby Junction with iron ore empties returning to Immingham from Scunthorpe on 6 May 1988. The second locomotive, No 37225, is still in standard BR corporate blue livery.** *John S. Whiteley*

unloading took place. This exercise was in connection with a proposed new rail link, to run south from Hawkhurst Moor and cross the Birmingham-London main line to join the former Kenilworth to Berkswell line at Burton Green, and the Coventry-Leamington line at Kenilworth Common. Trains would carry 1,950 tonnes of coal in 60-wagon trains, dispensing with 80 heavy lorry-loads. Class 58s Nos 58002 and 58041 powered the 'fact-finding' tours on different occasions, hauling just one coach.

Didcot power station was commemorated on 11 June 1988 when Class 58 No 58014 was named *Didcot Power Station* by Euro MP for Wiltshire, Dr Caroline Jackson. The locomotive was displayed with MGR hoppers, both displaying the Railfreight Coal sub-Sector black and yellow diamond markings.

In Staffordshire an era came to an end on 30 August 1988 with the running of the last train from British Industrial Sand's Oakamoor quarry, conveying sand to St Helens. In latter years the trains had generally been Class 20-hauled, and the last run was no exception, Nos 20120/32 providing the motive power. The line closed to passengers in 1965, but the section from Leek Brook Junction to Stoke will be retained to allow Tarmac's Caldon Low quarry to remain rail-served. All future output from Oakamoor will travel by road.

In Wales a new BSC spur from the Newport East Usk Junction-Uskmouth branch was opened on 19 August 1988, running to a mini-terminal adjacent to the Orb works. This spur will enable 80,000 tonnes of hot rolled steel coil to be delivered to the works direct from BSC's hot strip mills, eliminating 5,000 13-mile local lorry journeys a year.

Further west, at Coedbach washery, Class 37/5 locomotive No 37698 received the name *Coedbach* on 21 September 1988. Dating from August 1953, the British Coal washery, near Kidwelly, Dyfed, has the capacity to process 470,000 tonnes of anthracite each year by using opencast sites at Ffos Las and Gilfach Iago, output from the latter having been

being one of the benefits arising from Freightliner's merger with Railfreight's Speedlink sub-Sector. Trains now leave Coatbridge for Bristol Freightliner Terminal at 15.00 daily, arriving at 12.15 the next day, and trains leave Bristol at 14.00 and arrive at Coatbridge at 07.04 the following morning.

Redland was in the news again in May 1988 when its new aggregates terminal at Langley Junction came into operation with two workings each week from Mountsorrel, bringing Class 56s to the area for the first time. New rakes of Redland self-discharging hopper wagons, built at Standard Wagon, Heywood, are used on these trains. Power for the hydraulics on these wagons is provided by a Lister diesel engine mounted on the end wagon in the rake.

During 1988 Foster Yeoman introduced a regular Class 59-hauled aggregates working between Merehead and Crawley, and in July Tiphook PLC commenced delivery of 50 new hopper wagons for the company's services. These wagons, intended for the new Crawley service, were built by Arbel-Fauvet in France.

In the Midlands, a new Railfreight contract with ICI was marked by a naming ceremony at ICI's Hindlow plant in Derbyshire, on 23 June 1988. Class 37/5 locomotive No 37688 was named *Great Rocks* for the occasion. The new contract involves two limestone trains per day from Tunstead Quarry to Hindlow, each comprising 17 ICI hopper wagons with a total payload of 800 tonnes. It is expected that around 550,000 tonnes will be conveyed annually, and Buxton-based 'dedicated' Class 37s are used on these trains.

Further south, in the West Midlands, 'fact-finding' tours were organised by Railfreight in June 1988, during which local councillors were invited to view merry-go-round (MGR) coal operations at Daw Mill Colliery near Nuneaton, and at the CEGB's Ratcliffe-on-Soar power station where

60

screened and reduced at Cwmmawr. An £8 million modernisation programme commenced in 1980 in which rail sidings were renewed, enabling most of the plant's output to travel to customers by rail using the Coedbach-Kidwelly line, closed since 1964.

November 1988 saw the end of freight operations to the ARC quarry at Blodwell, in Mid-Wales. Both Class 37 and 31 locomotives were used on this duty during its last year of operation. The line to the quarry ran from Gobowen, over ex-GWR and Cambrian metals, and loaded trains from the quarry ran to Bescot for use by the Regional Civil Engineer at Crewe.

On the LMR, a major development is in force at Willesden Brent Yard. It is scheduled to be the inland terminal for Railfreight Distribution sub-Sector traffic using the Channel Tunnel and developments include the creation of HM Customs facilities. Some sidings have already been renewed and new

Above right:
During 1988, Foster Yeoman commenced operation of a regular Class 59-hauled service between Merehead and Crawley in Sussex using the new Tiphook aggregate hoppers which were delivered from July for workings to the southeast. Class 59 No 59003 *Yeoman Highlander* is seen here with the new wagons, on a return working from Crawley on 13 October 1988, at Acton Wells Junction.
*Brian Morrison*

Right:
Class 81 ac electric locomotive No 81011 leaves the Ford plant at Dagenham and approaches Dagenham Dock station with the 12.43 'Silcock Express' car-carrying train to Garston, on Merseyside. It is seen passing the original London, Tilbury & Southend Railway signalbox which dates from 1901. Prior to electrification of the North London link, these trains were Class 47-hauled. *Ken Brunt*

sidings up to 750m in length are planned. At present, 22 sidings at Brent can handle electrified services and, at the time of writing, four more are being equipped. Motive power to be seen on Railfreight Distribution services at Willesden includes Classes 31, 37 and 47, as well as all the ac electric locomotive classes. Willesden No 9 signalbox has been renamed 'Willesden Brent Sidings' and, in line with the sectorisation of infrastructure, sports Railfreight Distribution symbols on the outside. The first Class 86 ac electric locomotive to be modified for Railfreight Distribution work was No 86501 *Talyllyn*, although it was outshopped in BR Main Line livery (similar to the original InterCity Sector livery).

On the Freightliner scene, Tilbury, on the Anglian Region, held a 'first million' celebration on 26 September 1988, during which Class 37/0 No 37059 was named *Port of Tilbury* at Tilbury Riverside station. One million containers have been handled by Tilbury in its 19 years of operation, and in the year leading up to the naming Tilbury handled 88,000 containers.

At Parkeston Quay, Sealink has gained the short-sea Freightliner business at the expense of Felixstowe and, from January 1989, this operation involved foreign vessels, crossing from Zeebrugge.

A new Freightliner depot was under construction on Teesside, at the time of writing, on 15 acres of land leased from ICI, Wilton. It is scheduled for operation in 1989 replacing existing facilities at Stockton.

Above:
**Hauling a nuclear flask from Dungeness power station, bound eventually for Sellafield in Cumbria, Class 33/0 No 33031 passes the remains of Lydd Town station on 4 August 1988.** *Brian Morrison*

Below:
**This view, taken at Par on 29 March 1988, shows Railfreight, Network SouthEast and InterCity liveries. A down ballast train approaches the station in the care of Railfreight Class 37/5 No 37673 piloting Network SouthEast-liveried Class 50 No 50025** *Invincible* **which had failed. In the background, the 08.28 Penzance-Paddington HST working heads eastwards.** *Michael J. Collins, BA*

# 8

# Parcels, Newspapers and Post Office Traffic

## Parcels

On 3 October 1987, Class 47/4 No 47522 was repainted in LNER apple green livery at BRML Doncaster, and to mark the occasion the locomotive was named *Doncaster Enterprise*. It was suggested at the time that this locomotive's livery could be the forerunner of a Parcel's Sector scheme, but no futher locomotives have been so treated. No 47522 was seen on a variety of non-Parcels Sector duties during 1988, on at least one occasion substituting for a Class 142 Pacer unit. In May 1988, on closure of Gateshead depot, *Doncaster Enterprise* was reallocated to Stratford, although remaining one of the six Class 47s allocated to ECML Parcels duties, the others being Nos 47523/72/74/80/85. Parcels trains were also a preserve of the Class 45 'Peaks' in their latter days — indeed, in June 1988, Nos 45103/06/07/10/13/28/41 were allocated to the Parcels Sector.

During 1988, the Parcels Sector's Red Star business held about 12% of the parcels distribution market in Britain with heavy competition coming from the Post Office's Datapost service, Securicor and TNT. A total of 520 stations have Red Star parcels points, but further growth is proving slow.

## Newspapers

Sadly, 1988 marked the end of exclusive newspaper trains on BR when, from 10 July, the newspaper operation ceased. The principal reason for this was the restructuring of the newspaper industry's distribution requirements that had been in progress ever since the News International Group, whose publications include *The Sun* and *The Times*, rejected rail in favour of road distribution from its Wapping plant early in 1986, losing the Parcels Sector £9 million a year in revenue. The crippling blow came later when the Mirror Group also reverted to road distribution, costing BR a further £5 million in lost annual revenue, and tipping the business into unprofitability. The news that services were to cease resulted in railway enthusiasts arriving at such diverse locations as Manchester and Waterloo during the night to see and photograph the final workings.

The cessation of traffic made many vehicles surplus to requirements, 230 vans being scheduled for withdrawal. Withdrawals involved six types of van — NCV (9 vehicles), NDV (41), NJV (2), NKV (146), NMV (13), and NPV (19). The vehicles had been allocated to Manchester Longsight (87), Cambridge (33), Cardiff Canton (28), Bristol Marsh Junction (22), Heaton (15), Old Oak Common (14), Derby (12), Ilford (8), Eastleigh (4), Euston (3), Brighton (3), Ipswich (1) and Inverness (1). These withdrawals were particularly ironic, since only a year previously Ilford had converted the first Class 114 DTS, No 54034, to DTP No 55933, and turned it out in smart blue livery with 'Newspapers' lettering emblazoned upon it. Roller doors for ease of loading were a feature of the design.

## Post Office Traffic

The painting of certain Class 128 DMLVs in Post Office red livery took place in 1988 following the removal of asbestos at Vic Berry's of Leicester. The vehicles were overhauled at BRML Doncaster. The bright yellow front end, combined with the Post Office red sides with their yellow stripes offered a certain attraction! No 55992, together with No 55991, was once a familiar sight on the London Division of the WR working Reading-Paddington duties, and it regularly worked on the West Drayton-Colnbrook branch in the early 1960s. All five vehicles were reallocated to the main Parcels Sector DMU depot at Cambridge.

Modification of some Class 114 DMUs for Post Office work took place at Derby RTC in 1988, including the fitting of Leyland TL11 engines and painting in Post Office red livery. The first to be modified, set No T001 (cars Nos 54902/55932) was outshopped in

Below:
**The Saturday morning vans train from Bristol Malago Vale to Old Oak Common passes through West Drayton station in West London powered by Class 50 No 50037 *Illustrious*, with 19 vehicles in tow.** *Brian Morrison*

Top:
**Hauled by Class 47/4 No 47451, instead of being under their own power, a Metro-Cammell Class 101 unit, comprising cars Nos 53373 and 51439, and a Derby-built Class 114 unit form a down parcels train, seen approaching Ely on 25 March 1988.** *Brian Morrison*

Above:
**Class 308/2 three-car parcels unit No 308995 ascends Brentwood bank towards Ingrave summit on a rainy 16 April 1988, heading for Southend Victoria. The five units which originally made up this type were introduced five years ago when the Driving Trailer Standard vehicle of each was converted into a Driving Trailer Luggage Van, and the Trailer Composite coach of the original four-car Class 308/4 was removed. Only three units now remain in service.** *Brian Morrison*

March. Roller shutter doors have been fitted to both vehicles.

From May 1988, overnight Travelling Post Office (TPO) trains from Manchester to Dover began. Avoiding cross-London transfers, these trains convey first-class mail via Redhill, Reading and Birmingham. Class 319 units are used over the 'Thameslink' route to link into the new TPO workings at Luton and Redhill.

To commemorate the new service, and to celebrate 150 years of TPOs, Class 73/1 No 73138 was named *Post Haste*, with the nameplate being cast in Post Office style lettering. Ironically, this new service is normally hauled by a Class 47 locomotive and

No 73138 has been seen on a variety of duties varying from Speedlink freight to Bournemouth line expresses.

Coinciding with the anniversary celebrations, BR and the Royal Mail agreed a five-year contract worth around £200 million to carry letters by rail, including performance-related bonuses. There are, at present, 250 mail trains daily, carrying 60% of the 51 million letters posted daily in Britain — a considerable amount of sorting is carried out en route!

Other changes to the TPO network which have occurred since May 1988 include new London-Shrewsbury (and return) workings, a new service between London and Swansea, and the

Left:
**Sporting the red 'Royal Mail' livery, a BR Derby-built Class 114 DMU, formed of DMBP cars Nos 55932 and 54902, is pictured at Crewe on 28 April 1988.** *John Scrace*

Below:
**The first of the 10 Class 419 Motor Luggage Vans (MLVs) to be painted into 'Royal Mail' red livery was No 9004 seen here at the Central Section terminus side of London Bridge station in the early hours of 11 November 1988 waiting to be loaded with mail for Redhill.** *Brian Morrison*

Top:
**The 19.22 TPO from Penzance draws to a halt at Exeter St Davids station in order to pick up more mail to be sorted as the train proceeds through the night to its Paddington destination. It will be powered throughout by Class 50 No 50002 *Superb*.** *Colin J. Marsden*

Above:
**Class 127 Derby-built DPU No 920, comprising cars Nos M55966/67, stands outside Doncaster's repair workshops on 11 July 1987. Displaying the legend 'Newspapers' on one car and 'Express Parcels' on the other, this unit carries BR green livery.** *Peter Marsh*

Top right:
**BRCW BG 90mph newspaper packing van No 80768 (built in 1955) stands at BRML Wolverton on 30 January 1988 awaiting attention.** *Brian Morrison*

Right:
**In the distinctive red, white, blue and grey livery of the Network SouthEast Sector, Class 47/4 No 47582 *County of Norfolk* awaits departure from Paddington on 16 January 1988 with the 00.20 newspaper train to Bristol Temple Meads. Less than six weeks later, all dedicated trains of this type had ceased running following BR's loss of its main newspaper transportation contracts.** *Brian Beer*

replacement of the London-Penzance TPO (running via Bristol) with the 'Great West TPO', running over the Berks & Hants line with new arrival times to assist deliveries. In addition, more letters can now be handled on the Derby-Bristol TPO service which has also been extended to Penzance. This train now connects with the London-Plymouth TPO at Plymouth. A further new service that has been introduced is the 'Yorkshire TPO', connecting London St Pancras and Newcastle, with connections from Bristol and the Midlands. To link up with the Derby-Peterborough-East Anglia TPO service, it is planned to reintroduce a King's Cross-Newcastle TPO over the ECML. The London-Carlisle service, over the WCML, has been extended to Glasgow with faster timings being introduced over this route.

# 9

# The Settle & Carlisle Line

The decision on whether or not to close the Settle & Carlisle route still hung in the balance at the end of 1988.

During 1987, passenger figures for the line had increased for the fifth year in succession. It proved to be one of Provincial's better revenue earners relative to expenditure (62p revenue being taken for every £1 in costs) making the closure case appear insubstantial, but the major stumbling block remained Ribblehead Viaduct and other supposedly crumbling structures on the line.

In August 1987, the Amey Roadstone Co (ARC) suggested to BR that limestone from Ribblehead quarry could be conveyed over the Settle & Carlisle line to desulphurised power stations at Drax and the proposed West Burton (Notts) and Fawley (Hants) power stations. The power station requirement would be around 350,000 tonnes annually, but would not come on stream until 1993 at the earliest.

On 30 January 1988 InterCity, in conjunction with Hertfordshire Railtours, took its first HST charter train over the line, and it ran fully laden with 440 passengers. The train left St Pancras at 07.45 and, after calling at Derby, traversed the Hope Valley route and ran into Manchester Victoria. It then proceeded to Hellifield and Settle, arriving at Appleby ahead of schedule. After a short break, the charter train continued to Carlisle and returned to St Pancras via the Carlisle-Newcastle line, the ECML and Sheffield. By popular demand a similar, previously unscheduled, tour was arranged on 9 April — proof of the line's popularity with railway enthusiasts. While on the Settle & Carlisle line, the HST charter passed Class 50s Nos 50008 *Thunderer* and 50034 *Furious* heading south from Carlisle on a Taunton-Carlisle railtour. The day was typically Cumbrian — cold and wet — which did not please lineside photographers.

On 16 May 1988, the Minister of Transport announced that a final decision on the future of the line would be made in November. The hope was that a private buyer could be found. Despite the previously quoted figures it was claimed by BR that the line was losing £1 million annually and that repair work required on the Ribblehead Viaduct was still an expensive problem. It was announced that BR would be required, from 30 November, to operate the line for a further four months (pending a buyer being found), after which closure of the line would take place. This deadline was then extended to May.

During October 1988, buses replaced trains from Horton-in-Ribblesdale to Garsdale when track was lifted — but it was not what it seemed. BR engineers were assessing the cost of repairing Ribblehead Viaduct, which was not as much as expected, at the same time taking advantage of the situation to renew track at Selside —

Below:
**Class 47/4 No 47492 rolls off the Settle & Carlisle line at Settle Junction, on 28 May 1988, with a Carlisle-Leeds service. In the foreground can be seen the line to Carnforth and Morecambe.**
*Les Nixon*

somewhat strange for a line that was, at the time, pending closure.

Throughout and during 1987 and 1988, the line continued to be used for WCML diversions at weekends due to engineering work on the electrified route. BR's original plan for coping with WCML diversions following closure of the Settle & Carlisle line involved the tortuous Cumbrian Coast line, but this has now been abandoned in favour of bus substitutions and diversions via the ECML.

Above left:
**On 29 October 1988, a five-car DMU special is pictured at Newbiggin returning from Carlisle, with car No W53093 leading. Class 101 and 108 units were operating Carlisle-Leeds services at this time.** *Les Nixon*

Left:
**A southbound excursion, headed by Class 47 No 47567 *Red Star*, and comprising the 'Raspberry Ripple' stock, passes Lazonby on 25 June 1988. The station and goods shed can be seen in the background.** *Les Nixon*

Below:
**BR in conjunction with Hertfordshire Railtours operated 'HST Specials' over the Settle & Carlisle route from St Pancras during 1988 and, on 26 November 1988, an excursion is seen near Helwith Bridge amongst typical S&C scenery.** *Les Nixon*

Many enthusiasts have fond memories of the Settle & Carlisle line, both from travelling along it or from chasing steam specials by car along the long winding roads which follow the line as far as Ribblehead. Diesel enthusiasts will remember the Class 25s, 'Peaks' and 'Whistlers' in particular as they pounded up the banks, over the viaducts and through the tunnels.

Right:
**Steam specials were still abundant in 1988 over the Settle & Carlisle route and on some occasions these were accompanied by ex-Class 25 ETHELs for train heating purposes. On 12 November 1988 ex-LMS Stanier Class '8F' No 48151 is seen at Eden Lacey with ETHEL 2. The '8F', looking resplendent in its black livery was scheduled to come off this train at Hellifield.** *Les Nixon*

Below:
**The infamous *Mallard*, 'A4' No 4468, glides to a halt, short of steam, with an Eaglescliffe-Newcastle-Carlisle-Leeds-York excursion on 27 August 1988. Since the reprieve for this picturesque line we can thankfully look forward to more impressive scenes such as this for a few more years.** *Les Nixon*

# 10
# Gone But Not Forgotten

During the latter part of 1987 and throughout 1988, certain locomotive classes, types of trains and previously common sights have sadly disappeared. The locomotives and units that have gone were covered earlier, as were the newspaper trains, but perhaps some of the locations and workings mentioned here will bring back a few memories.

## Locomotive Depots

### Lincoln

The end came for Lincoln depot on 4 October 1987 following the introduction of the Class 150 Sprinters to the area's services. The depot will be remembered for its Class 105 allocation, its abundance of Class 114 Derby Heavyweight units and, going back to the 1960s its allocation of three Class 31s, Nos 5800/01/02.

### Cricklewood

Cricklewood was another depot to close during the period under review, and will be remembered for its substantial allocation of DMUs, Class 45 'Peaks' and, back in the 1960s, Class 27 diesels.

Above left:
**Standing outside Lincoln traction depot just prior to closure on 25 September 1987 can be seen Class 31/4 No 31438 and the leading car, No 53036, of a Derby Class 114 DMU set.** *Brian Morrison*

Left:
**A wide-angle view of the famous Cricklewood traction repair depot shortly prior to closure, showing Class 317 EMU No 317325.**
*Brian Morrison*

## Gateshead

This well known depot finally closed for main line locomotive maintenance in May 1988. Best known for its allocation of 'Deltics' and Class 46 'Peaks', it was always an interesting depot to visit with its variety of main line motive power including Class 31s, 37s and 47s, in particular the early series generator-equipped Class 47/4s. There never appeared to be a great number of locomotives on shed, such as at Tinsley or Toton, but at least Class 03s lasted until four months prior to the depot's closure, and they were always a welcome sight.

## March

This depot, situated in the Fens, will always be remembered for its predominance of Class 31s and 37s. In December 1987 large numbers of withdrawn locomotives were stored there for recovery of components, and every day saw new arrivals. Stored locomotives included Class 03 shunters from Norwich and many Class 45 'Peaks'. However bleak this location always seemed, we shall certainly not forget it.

## Hull (Botanic Gardens)

At one time Hull sported two depots, Botanic Gardens and Dairycoates. Some years ago Dairycoates closed and many will remember the Class 14 'Paxmans' being stored in the depot's roundhouse, but the DMU depot at Botanic Gardens has also now closed, bringing an end to diesel maintenance in the city. The depot will principally be remembered for its Class 101, 108, 123 and 124 DMUs.

## St Leonards

Home of the slim-line 'Hastings' DEMUs, St Leonards housed locomotive repair shops as well as having an allocation of Class 201, 202, 203, 205 and 207 DEMUs. The site comprised two main DEMU sheds, one for maintenance and one a running shed, separated by a distance of about 100yd, and Class 33s could often be seen stabled there.

Below:
**The once-extensive yards at Severn Tunnel Junction closed on 12 October 1987, with Speedlink and other workings being transferred to East Usk yard and Cardiff Tidal sidings. In August 1987, just a few months prior to closure, two freight trains leave the yard with eastbound workings headed by English Electric Class 37/0 locomotives Nos 37250 and 37257.**
*Brian Morrison*

## Carlisle (Kingmoor)

In its latter years Kingmoor was used for storing withdrawn motive power, and was also responsible for stripping components from withdrawn Class 47s. The depot, situated on the down side of the WCML about two miles north of Carlisle station, will be remembered by modern traction enthusiasts for its allocation of Class 25s and Class 40s. The closure of Kingmoor has meant that fuelling, servicing and maintenance of the area's Class 08 fleet is now undertaken at Upperby depot, about a mile south of Carlisle station.

## Marshalling Yards

### Margam Hump Yard

After 25 years in use, the 52 sidings comprising the Margam Hump Yard were closed in 1987. Adjacent to the yard was Margam depot, where a good variety of motive power could always be found, ranging from Class 14 'Paxmans' and Class 52 'Westerns' in the 1960s to Class 37s, 45s, 47s and 56s in the 1980s. When opened, Margam was one of the largest and most modern hump marshalling yards in the country — indeed, over its 180-acre area there were 33 miles of rail! Another of Britain's major marshalling yards has succumbed to modernisation.

### Severn Tunnel Junction

On 10 October 1987, the yards and servicing depot at Severn Tunnel Junction were finally closed. Prior to closure of the yard, track was being lifted by use of a 12-ton crane. The depot/stabling point has always proved to be an interesting location to visit over the years and has provided a good variety of motive power. Following the closure of the depot, Departmental shunter No 97806 (ex-No 09017) was stabled at Sudbrook Pumping Station where it is still kept for use on the Severn Tunnel emergency train.

## Signalling

### Midland Main Line Semaphores

Kettering station signalbox was one of many boxes taken out of use following the resignalling of the Midland main line. Fortunately, this particular box has been preserved. The semaphores

Below:
**HST unit No 253026, forming the 10.35 Nottingham-St Pancras, passes Wigston South Junction signalbox prior to completion of the Leicester resignalling scheme.** *Brian Morrison*

Bottom:
**During 1988 the old-style clay hoods were replaced by new CDA hoppers constructed at Doncaster Works. In this view at Lostwithiel on 24 August 1987, Class 37/5 No 37671 shunts the yard, packed with old clay hoods, while Class 50 No 50019 *Ramillies* passes with the 11.45 Paddington-Penzance.**
*Brian Morrison*

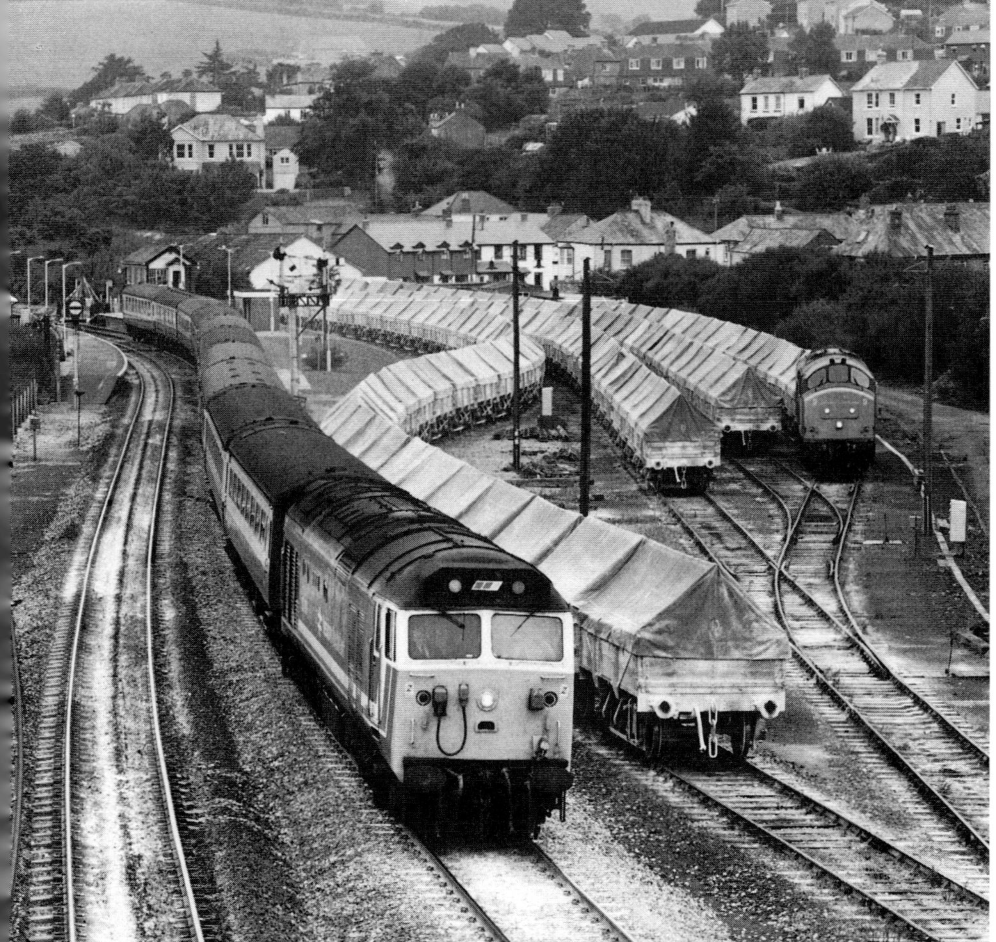

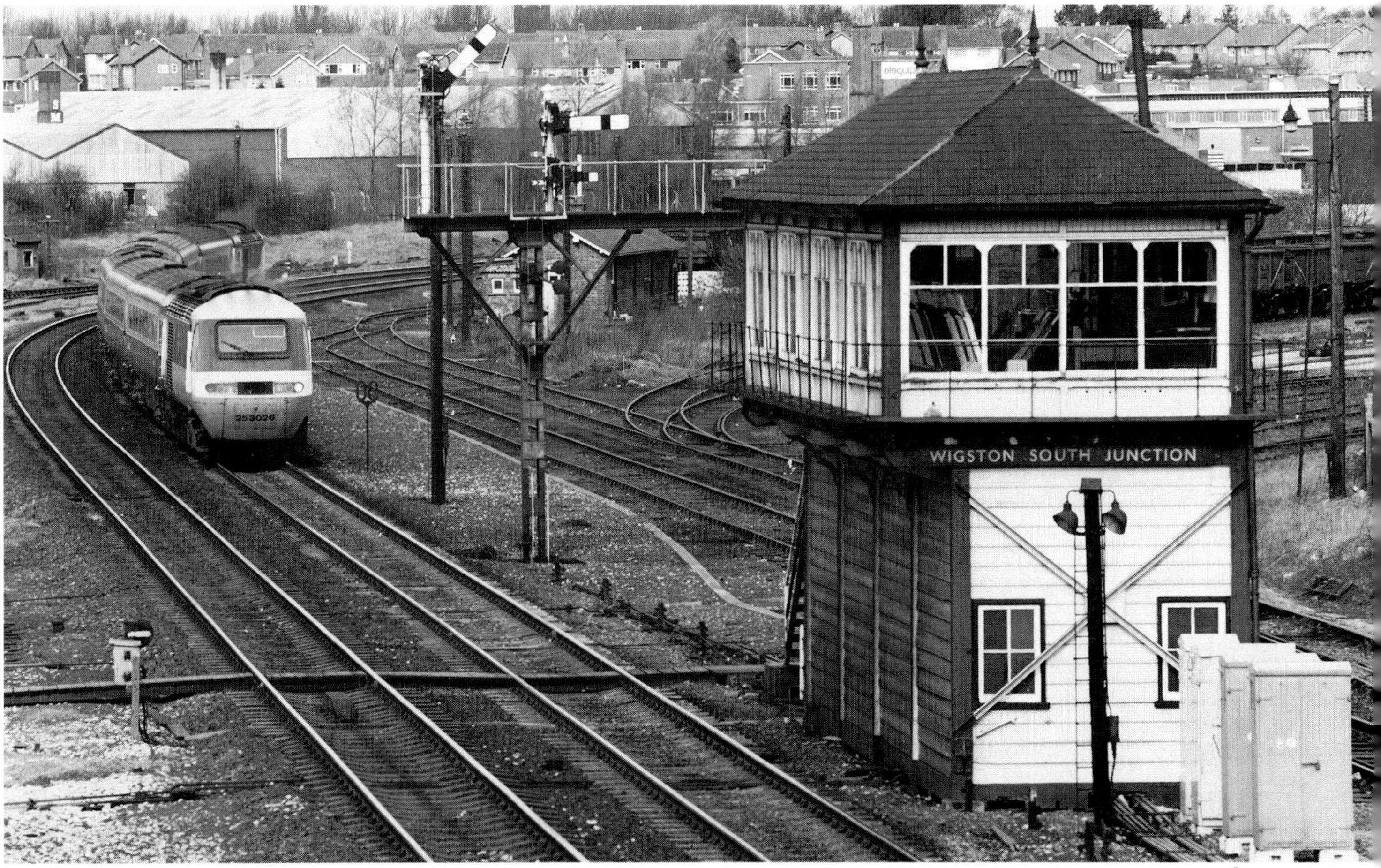


on this route will be sadly missed by enthusiasts, and their presence proved to be an attraction for many railway photographers. The Midland main line has thus lost two of its most characteristic features during the period under review, the 'Peak' class diesels and its semaphore signals. Perhaps one day electrification will lead to even more radical changes.

## Wagons

### *ECC Clay Hoods*

In 1988 the old 'clay hoods', a feature of the china clay trains in the West Country, were replaced with more modern wagons built at RFS Engineering, Doncaster. However, there were some initial problems with the new wagons, giving the old 'clay hoods' a 'stay of execution'. Enthusiasts made special sorties into the West Country just to photograph the china clay trains at places such as Burngullow, Drinnick Mill, Carne Point and Lostwithiel, and back in the 1970s there was no finer sight than that of a

Below:
**The North Trans-Pennine passenger workings were all locomotive-hauled until May 1988, when some workings** were taken over by Sprinters. On 19 April 1988 one of the remaining Class 47/4 'Generators', No 47407, is seen near Earlestown with the 15.03 Liverpool Lime Street-Newcastle. At this time the locomotive was named *Aycliffe* but these plates have since been transferred to No 47452. *Peter Hill*

Right:
**Locomotive-hauled passenger services on the Newquay branch in Cornwall are a thing of the past, London services now being formed of HST units. During the last summer of locomotive-hauled working, in 1987, Network SouthEast Sector Class 50 No 50032 *Courageous* traverses the branch near St Blazey with the 17.17 service from Newquay to Plymouth.** *Brian Morrison*

Class 52 'Western' with a long train of 'hoods'. China clay trains are currently hauled by Class 37s.

## Duties

### *Loco-Hauled Trains on the Newquay Branch*

The last scheduled locomotive-hauled service to Newquay in Cornwall ran on 4 October 1987. This was a special tour from Paddington appropriately powered by Class 50 traction. For the occasion, Nos 50034 *Furious* and 50035 *Ark Royal* provided the power. Both locomotives sported Network SouthEast livery. IC125 units now generally work these services and the Class 50s that once operated on the line will be sadly missed. One wonders how many of this popular locomotive class will enter the ranks of diesel preservation.

# 11
# Diesel Preservation

Diesel preservation continued to thrive during 1987 and 1988, both on private lines, at the National Railway Museum and at Crewe Heritage Centre. This brief review covers some of the events which took place during the period in this popular area of railway enthusiasm.

## Locomotives

### No D1041 Western Prince

No D1041 *Western Prince*, a Class 52 diesel-hydraulic locomotive, left Crewe Works on 4 February 1988 resplendent in its early maroon livery with yellow buffer beams and no yellow warning panel. A brass plaque was placed above each numberplate to commemorate its refurbishment by BREL. The locomotive was in excellent condition, both mechanically and visually. It was displayed at Crewe Heritage Centre during the summer, with subsequent appearances being made at the 'Winchfield 150' celebrations, the Severn Valley Railway and the Keighley & Worth Valley Railway, before returning to Crewe for the winter. It is hoped that this fine locomotive will soon be back in action on the East Lancashire Railway.

### No D200

After its final run from Liverpool Street to York via Norwich, the last Class 40 remaining on BR, No D200, came to rest at the NRM on 16 April 1988, after 30 years of reliable service. On its final journey to York, it was accompanied by the 'raspberry ripple' set of open firsts, and no ETHEL was in attendance. No D200 had 'whistled' for the last time in BR service.

### No D100 Sherwood Forester

The green-liveried Class 45/0 'Peak', No D100 *Sherwood Forester*, (ex-No 45060) appeared for all to see at the Basingstoke gala celebrations on 26 and 27 September 1987, sporting 'The Robin Hood' headboard. Restoration to its original pristine condition was carried out at Tinsley TMD. No doubt, we shall be seeing more 'Peaks' on the preservation scene in years to come.

### Class 08

The Brechin Railway's Class 08 shunter, No D3059 (ex-13059), was repainted to BR green during 1988 and named *Brechin City* after the Scottish football club.

### Class 25

The Llangollen Railway acquired its first Class 25 diesel in 1987, Beyer Peacock-built No 25279 (ex-No D7629). This was one of the last of the class in traffic, having been withdrawn in March 1987. Its final allocation was Crewe diesel depot. Work will now commence on bringing the locomotive back to its former glory. Six more Class 25s were sold for

Above left:
**On 31 October 1987 Class 47/4 No 47553, newly painted into InterCity Sector livery, shares Crewe Works paint shop with preserved Class 52 'Western' No D1041 *Western Prince*, awaiting painting into maroon livery before going to the East Lancashire Railway at Bury.** *Brian Morrison*

Left:
**The Basingstoke gala weekend on 26 and 27 September 1987 featured, as one of its exhibits, newly-painted preserved Class 27 No 27059 in BR corporate blue livery. During the following month this locomotive was seen operating on the Severn Valley Railway on the occasion of their Diesel Weekend.** *Peter Marsh*

preservation in 1987 (most having had their asbestos removed prior to being released). They are Nos 25059 (Keighley & Worth Valley Railway), 25173 (Dean Forest Railway), 25244 (Swanage Railway), 25191 and 25278 (North Yorkshire Moors Railway) and 25904 (Severn Valley Railway). No 25067 (ex-D5217) has been preserved on the Mid-Hants Railway since 1985.

### Class 27

During 1988, the Class 27 Locomotive Group's pride and joy, No 27001, became the first member of the class to operate in preservation when, under its own power, it was driven on to and off a low-loader on its delivery to Brechin, from Montrose. It later worked engineer's trains on the Brechin Railway. In 1987, No 27005 was purchased by the Scottish Railway Preservation Group. It was scheduled for the Bo'ness & Kinneil Railway after removal of asbestos by MC Processors, Springburn, Glasgow. It is planned to return the locomotive to traffic as No D5351, sporting its original green livery, after minor repairs have been carried out.

No 27059, withdrawn in July 1987, appeared at the Basingstoke gala weekend on 26 and 27 September 1987 and at Tyseley on 4 October, on both occasions looking very smart indeed. On 10 and 11 October, No 27059 operated passenger services between Bridgnorth and Bewdley on the Severn Valley Railway. This locomotive received a final repaint at Eastfield following its withdrawal and it has been preserved by Sandwell District Council. It is based at the Birmingham Railway Museum (Tyseley).

Glasgow Springburn depot restored Class 27 No D5394 (ex-No 27050) to its original green livery prior to handing the locomotive over to the Strathspey Railway. Hopefully yet further examples of this popular class will be saved for preservation.

## Events

### Bury Diesels

On 1 and 2 October 1988, the East Lancashire Railway staged a successful gala weekend. Operating for the first time since preservation were North British shunter No D2767, Class 14 'Paxman' No D9531, Class 24 No D5054, Class 25 No 25909 and Class 35 'Hymek' No D7076. Also operating on the day were Class 40 No D345 (the largest locomotive on

Above:
**The Class 40 Preservation Society's locomotive, No 40145, is pictured at Summerseat, on the East Lancashire Railway, on a very dull 10 September 1988 with a Bury-Ramsbottom service.**
*Les Nixon*

show) and Class 42 'Warship' No D832 *Onslaught*. BR has stated that the ban on diesels still in capital stock working on preserved lines, imposed during the summer of 1988, is just a temporary measure.

### Crewe Heritage Centre

This centre, which has now become a permanent feature at Crewe, held a railway exhibition from 29 July to 4 September 1988. Originally, the first Class 47 diesel to be preserved was to have been No 47001 (ex-No D1521) which was to have been donated by BREL Crewe to the Heritage Centre. However, in the event it was No 47015 that was located there in June 1988. No 47001 has since found residence at the Heritage Centre.

Seven Advanced Passenger Trains (APT) vehicles, Nos 48103, 48606, 48603, 49002, 49006, 48602 and 48106, were moved to the Heritage Centre on 15 June 1988. Most vehicles of this ill-fated tilting train were cut up at Litchurch Lane Carriage Works, Derby, during 1987.

Below:
**On 16 August 1987, Class 42 'Warship' No D832 *Onslaught* leaves Bury for Ramsbottom with the 17.00 service. The locomotive was one of the three diesel-hydraulics operating on the East Lancashire Railway Gala Weekend on 1 and 2 October 1988 together with Class 14 'Paxman' No D9531 and Class 35 'Hymek' No D7076.**
*Tom Heavyside*

# 12
# Into the Future

What does the future hold for BR, its passengers and railway enthusiasts? New classes of locomotive and new multiple-units, all of futuristic designs, new railway systems similar to London's Docklands Light Railway in operation in many British towns and cities, new lines opening or old ones reopening, more electrification on BR and eventually the possibility of catching a train from virtually anywhere in Britain to almost anywhere in Europe.

## Class 60

The proposed design options for the new Class 60 Railfreight diesel locomotive were first revealed in August 1987. Drivers' sightlines dictated the size of the windows and the design had to meet international requirements for collision protection. The modern cab design of Class 58 and 59 was found to be suitable for the new Class 60. Originally, six manufacturers were invited to tender for construction of the new locomotive — General Motors, General Electric (USA), Brush, GEC, Northern Engineering Industries (in conjunction with two German firms), and Metro-Cammell.

Provisionally, Railfreight envisages the 100 Class 60s ordered to be allocated to the following sub-Sectors: Petroleum (17), Coal (42), Metals & Automotives (17), and Construction, including Channel Tunnel (20). The remaining four locomotives have yet to be allocated. The introduction of the Class 60 fleet will allow the reallocation of Class 37 and 56 locomotives to other duties, in turn allowing the withdrawal of over 200 Class 20s, 33s and 47s. Allowing for its anticipated superior availability, one Class 60 should be able to undertake the work of four Class 20s.

A mock-up of the new locomotive appeared on view at the launch of Railfreight's new image at Ripple Lane depot on 17 October 1987 and, on 17 May 1988, the BR Board announced that the Class 60 contract would go to Brush Traction Ltd of Loughborough. The contract for the 100 locomotives is valued at £120 million and delivery is scheduled to start in June 1989 at the rate of 40 locomotives per year. The Class 60 will be fitted with the eight-cylinder Mirrlees MB275 RT engine developing 3,100bhp, and Brush-designed bogies similar to the CP-series units employed on the Class 58.

Their first duty will be Channel Tunnel construction traffic from the Isle of Grain to Shakespeare Cliff, at present being operated by Class 33 locomotives. Later deliveries are expected to be allocated to the Metals & Automotives sub-Sector for Hunterston-Ravenscraig traffic and Petroleum workings in South Humberside at present operated by double-headed Class 37s. We look forward, with a degree of excitement, to seeing the first of these new diesels in traffic.

## Class 158 'Express Sprinter'

Due to commence delivery in May 1989 are the Class 158 'Express Sprinters'. The bodies are being built at BREL Derby Litchurch Lane and the bogies at Derby Locomotive Works. The initial order was for 194 vehicles, with an option for further units if desired. The Class 158s are for use on long-distance cross-country routes, and are designed to operate at up to 90mph. The first services to receive these units are planned to be main line Provincial routes in Scotland. Eventually, the new units will take over services such as North Trans-Pennine, Cardiff-Portsmouth and Norwich-Birmingham, releasing Class 156 Super Sprinters for routes such as the Cambrian Coast and Manchester-Blackpool. The new Class 158 'Express Sprinters' should reduce running times considerably, trimming an hour off the Birmingham-Norwich timing, 28min off Sheffield-Blackpool, and 45min off the Manchester-Norwich schedule.

The Class 158 units will be all-standard class, although a section of each unit will be closed off providing greater comfort for passengers willing to pay a small surcharge.

## Class 165 'Networker Turbo'

The Class 165 'Networker Turbo' is intended to fulfil the principal requirement for DMUs on Network SouthEast services. Planned areas of operation are the Chiltern lines and Thames Valley services.

Other projected DMU types under consideration include Class 160, for use in the West Midlands if electrification of WMPTE services is not forthcoming, and Class 161 (single car units), for Provincial Sector rural services.

## Class 465 'Networker' EMU

The testbed for the 'Networker', in the form of the Class 457 EMU (developed from the Class 210 DEMU as noted in an earlier chapter), arrived at Strawberry Hill M&EE depot on 20 June 1988. The first Class 457 unit, No 7001, has been fitted with Brush three-phase ac traction motors and another vehicle, on test in Class 455 unit No 5920, has been fitted with GEC motors — a new innovation for BR EMUs. Evaluation tests are being carried out in preparation for these motors being used in the new Class 465.

The design of the 'Networker' was unveiled at Victoria station on 1 December 1987, and the new units are scheduled for Network South-East's Kent services from October 1990 and for Essex services from May 1992. The Kent units will be fitted for third-rail 750V dc power collection, and the Essex units will gain their power from the 25kV ac overhead catenary. Maximum operating speeds are expected to be 75mph for Kent and 100mph for Essex services. The units will be fitted with plug-type doors and high-backed seating. Delivery is expected to commence in May 1990 subject to authorisation and the placement of orders. We look forward to seeing these 1990s trains taking over from the dated stock at present used in Kent and Essex.

## Light Rapid Transit Schemes

Cities and towns all over Britain have been submitting schemes for Light Rapid Transit (LRT) systems following the success of the DLR in London. Places such as Manchester, Bristol, Nottingham, Leeds, Southampton and even Bournemouth are keen to invest in contemporary 'tramway' systems.

Greater Manchester PTE has applied for a grant towards the cost of building a system over the Manchester Victoria-Bury and Manchester Deansgate-Altrincham lines. This scheme would involve converting BR lines to LRT operation, and would include street-level running through Manchester city centre between Victoria and Piccadilly stations. The route length of the scheme would total 19 miles.

In Bristol, a LRT system has been agreed with Hawker Siddeley (partnered by Balfour Beatty) and Advanced Transport for Avon (ATA). Again the use of BR rights of way is being incorporated into the scheme, from the outskirts of Bristol to the city centre. Construction is due to start early in 1989, and is scheduled for completion two years later. This scheme is also intended to include street-level running.

West Yorkshire PTA is hoping to fund its own LRT system along an 11½km route from the centre of Leeds to the east of the city. The first phase is expected to cost around £27 million and is intended to link a terminus near Leeds Town Hall with both Cross Gates and Seacroft, via the Headrow and Quarry Hill — 8½km of the route being segregated from other traffic.

Thirteen stations are proposed for the line to Seacroft, and two for the spur to Cross Gates. A further spur has also been proposed to Colton (costing around £11 million) — with five stations being provided on the 3km route. Later extensions are envisaged to Holt Park, via Headingley, and to the south of Leeds — even a tunnel to cross the city centre has been suggested! Another area actively considering LRT is the West Midlands. Plans envisage an extensive system between Birmingham and Wolverhampton, largely exploiting disused BR routes.

The large number of LRT schemes presently under consideration casts some doubt on the wisdom of the wholesale destruction of Britain's tram and trolleybus systems during the 1950s and 1960s.

## The 'Battersea Bullet'

Three four-car EMUs are to be built to operate a privately-owned rail service across the River Thames. These units, ordered from BREL by the Battersea Leisure Group, are to be known as the 'Battersea Bullets' and they will operate between Victoria station and Battersea. The trains will be the first to be built by BREL for private operation using BR metals. A 'Palace of Entertainment' is being created by the owners of Alton Towers leisure park in Staffordshire and this will occupy the site of Battersea power station. The new leisure centre opens in 1990 and it is anticipated that half the five million visitors expected annually will use the 'Battersea Bullet' service. BREL York Works will build

the bodies for these units and the bogies will be manufactured at Derby. The four-car units will be based on the Class 321 design, but will be equipped for third-rail dc current collection only.

## Tyne & Wear Metro Extension

Tyne & Wear PTA is studying the possibility of extending its successful Metro system to Sunderland, probably from Heyworth, via Washington. A Newcastle airport extension has already been approved by the PTA at a cost of £11 million, and this will partly adopt BR's freight branch to the ICI works at Callerton, but this has met with some local objections, causing the PTA to modify its proposals.

## Luton to Dunstable

By 1991 the Luton-Dunstable line could again be open to passenger traffic. Passenger services were originally withdrawn in 1965, and it has

Below:
**During the winter of 1988, the Network SouthEast Sector issued a poster proudly proclaiming that the 1923-dated Isle of Wight stock was to be replaced during 1989 — what they omitted to say was that the 'new' stock was originally built for the London Underground in 1938! These red-liveried trains, which comply with the Island's restricted loading gauge, were towed from West Ruislip LT depot to Strawberry Hill EMUD, prior to visiting BRML Eastleigh for work to be undertaken on them before shipment across the Solent. Some of these cars are seen in the yard at Strawberry Hill on 30 October 1988.** *Brian Morrison*

been suggested that the reopened route could link into the 'Thameslink' system.

## Paddington to Heathrow

Government approval has been given for a new 17-mile electrified route between Paddington and Heathrow Airport, connecting with the WR main line at Iver. It is intended that half the new route will be underground. It is proposed to use 16 four-car ac EMUs, and these trains will probably be maintained at Old Oak Common. The route is funded by BAA PLC (formerly British Airports Authority) and scheduled to open in 1993, when trains will run at 15min intervals from 05.00 to 23.30, the journey taking 17min. Following the completion of this scheme, it would be a relatively simple matter to extend the electrification to Reading from where it is expected that an electric service will be operating to Gatwick Airport using EMU stock similar to Class 319.

## London Underground in the 21st Century

London's Underground system has experienced a 60% increase in traffic over a five-year period up to 1988, and a 20-year improvement plan for the system is being considered.

A £500 million improvement scheme, involving complete modernisation of the Central Line and improvements to congested stations is already underway and plans for the Northern Line have considered the possibility of dividing the route into two separate networks. The updating of the Underground system will cost several billion pounds, and numerous options, some including BR involvement, have been drawn up for consideration. Proposals include extending the Bakerloo Line to serve developments in the London Docklands at Canary Wharf, a new system linking King's Cross and Victoria via Piccadilly Circus, and a BR scheme for a cross-London tunnel. Further schemes are for a fast 'figure-of-eight' line linking the major BR termini, and an extension of the Jubilee Line eastwards from Charing Cross to link Essex with the proposed BR route to Heathrow Airport. Many of these proposals would involve the building of new tunnels and there is little room left below London's busy streets because of the existing system and the Post Office underground railway. In addition there are the sewers, water and gas mains to contend with, apart from the many drawbacks with foundations, and the impact on buildings on the surface. Certainly something has to be done for the future and hopefully some of these proposals will reach fruition.

## The Channel Tunnel

The long-awaited Channel Tunnel is at last under construction and is scheduled to open in 1993.

Shakespeare Cliff, Dover, is the point at which the service tunnel will emerge and the site beside the Dover to Ashford line has been a hive of activity.

On 16 May 1988, two Class 33/0 locomotives were named on the Isle of Grain to mark the signing of an agreement between Railfreight and Transmanche-Link, the tunnel's builders, to transport concrete segments, required for the tunnel's construction, from the Isle of Grain to Shakespeare Cliff. No 33050 was named *Isle of Grain* and No 33051 received the name *Shakespeare Cliff*, and both locomotives are part of a fleet of 14 Class 33s dedicated to construction traffic during the three-year contract period. Three trains run daily, the maximum gross weight of each train being 2,192 tonnes. Other duties for these dedicated locomotives include the haulage of stone from Snowdown Colliery to Sevington, and the transportation of aggregates to Shakespeare Cliff from the Isle of Grain. Railfreight is responsible for the haulage of 75% of the tunnel's bulk materials. Unfortunately No 33050 *Isle of Grain* met with an accident at Snowdown Colliery on 5 August 1988 when, together with No 33038, it was struck by runaway wagons. Both locomotives were taken to Eastleigh Works and then to Stratford Major Depot where

Below:
**From 14-22 March 1987, DLR unit No 11, specially fitted with a pantograph, carried out public demonstration runs for the first time outside London. These runs were held at Debdale Park, Manchester, on a 1¼ mile-long stretch of freight-only line where a wooden platform incorporating a bus shelter had been erected. On 15 March, unit No 11 is seen passing the former Reddish motive power depot, the demonstrations being designated 'Project Light Rail'. One day in the future, Manchester will be running its own LRT system.** *Richard Fox*

No 33050 was stripped pending further examination. As a point of interest regarding dedicated locomotives, No 33051 *Shakespeare Cliff* was seen working a Gillingham-Preston parcels service on 16 and 18 August 1988!

Tests in connection with Channel Tunnel traffic resulted in Britain's longest train, totalling 900m in length, being run over the Corby-Manton Junction line in Leicestershire hauled by two Class 20 locomotives, with a Class 47 being used to supply additional brakeforce. The objective was to test the strength of radio signal transmissions in tunnels, and for this purpose the train was hauled repeatedly in and out of the 1¼-mile Corby tunnel. The train comprised 42 Mk 1 passenger coaches and Derby RTC's Test Car *Iris* during these successful tests.

During the early part of 1988, tenders went out for the design, manufacture and commissioning of complete shuttle trains for the Channel Tunnel service, comprising 40 locomotives and 500 vehicle transporters. The Euroshuttle consortium, led by Brush Electrical Machines of Britain, was invited to tender, along



with ANF-Industrie of France, ASEA Brown Boveri of Switzerland, BN Constructions Ferroviqires of Belgium, and BREL/GEC Transportation Projects Ltd.

One of the most controversial issues concerning the Channel Tunnel has been the proposal for a high-speed line from the Channel Tunnel to London. A further question has been the choice of London terminus for Channel Tunnel traffic.

Three options were put forward by BR for the high-speed link and initially as many as 42 options (quickly reduced to 10) were suggested for the London terminal.

Regarding the routes, proposals 1 and 2 would both pass through Longfield, Snodland, Hollingbourne and Charing to the tunnel, the first routed via Sidcup and the second via Bromley. The third proposal would also take a route from Bromley, via Borough Green and Pluckley, but would follow a more southerly course. Another option, involving the upgrading of the existing main line route via Orpington, Sevenoaks and Tonbridge has also been considered. It is widely felt that a purpose-built high-speed route will be required to reduce the journey time from London to Paris by 25min, bringing it down to around 2½hr.

Discussions began during the summer of 1988 concerning the building of a new international station at Ashford to serve Channel Tunnel traffic. Costs are estimated at around £23 million and the building would include HM Customs and Immigration facilities enabling Continental passengers to board and alight from trains at this location.

From 1993 onwards, some of us could well be catching trains from major cities in Britain to Paris and beyond, instead of having to cross the Channel by ferry or waiting for hours at our crowded airports.